MW01058339

*To Lindsay, Wesley & Lucy.*
*My story is so much better because of you.*
*Here's to all the adventures to come.*

The excellent cover illustrations were done by the amazingly-talented Chris Mostyn, who can be found and/or hired at ChrisMostyn.com

The stories in this book are true as far as I remember. However, some of them happened over ten years ago, so you'll have to forgive me if I've messed up the specifics. Wherever possible, I tried to verify the stories with the people who were there. In a few places I changed a detail or two. Because I *can*, that's why.

Stories I did not personally witness have, where possible, been verified by people who did. Those people may be liars though, because some people are liars.

ISBN: 978-0-9857364-0-8

LCCN: 2012941304

First Edition

# WE PUT A MAN ON THE MOON

## THOUGHTS ON LIVING A BETTER STORY

KYLE SCHEELE

# Contents

## SECTION 1: The Necessary Formalities

Author's Note
Second Author's Note
Third Author's Note
Preface
Introduction

## SECTION 2: The Good Stuff

Chapter 1:   Telling Lies to Children .......................................... 23
Chapter 2:   Everything You Know is Wrong ......................... 31
Chapter 3:   We Put a Man on the Moon ............................... 39
Chapter 4:   Cheating for Idiots .............................................. 47
Chapter 5:   No More Good Choices ...................................... 57
Chapter 6:   Prank Calling the President .............................. 65
Chapter 7:   The Kind of Stories You Want to Read ............. 75
Chapter 8:   Just Like the Movies ........................................... 83
Chapter 9:   Walking Down Hallways .................................... 91
Chapter 10:  Here Lies John Smith .......................................... 99
Chapter 11:  Timeless Classics ............................................... 107
Chapter 12:  The Value of Stories ........................................... 115
Chapter 13:  Tribute Band Groupies ..................................... 123
Chapter 14:  The Floor is Lava ............................................... 131
Chapter 15:  Choose Your Own Adventure ......................... 139
Chapter 16:  Urban Legends ................................................... 147
Chapter 17:  Picking Fights .................................................... 155
Chapter 18:  Trust the Process ............................................... 161
Chapter 19:  Conclusion ......................................................... 165

## SECTION 3: Odds & Ends

Would You Do Me a Favor?
About the Author
Acknowledgments

# SECTION 1

## The Necessary Formalities

# Author's Note

IF YOU ARE THE SORT OF PERSON WHO IS UNDER the impression that Santa Claus is real (which is a perfectly reasonable sort of impression to be under, so don't think I am saying anything at all regarding his realness or lack thereof), this book may not be for you. Particularly the first chapter of this book.

Consider yourself forewarned that a freight train of honesty is headed straight for you if you should decide to continue reading.

For the rest of you, carry on!

# —— Second Author's Note ——

WHY DO THEY CALL IT AN AUTHOR'S NOTE? Isn't the whole book sort of an Author's Note? I've always wondered that.

Anyway, if you are the sort of person who silently mouths the words you are reading, please stop, at least for the duration of this book. That kind of thing is annoying, and it makes the people around you uncomfortable, and I do not wish for people to be annoyed or uncomfortable around this book.

There is not really a reason to move your mouth at all unless you are reading the book aloud to someone. If you are doing this, you should be aware that people who need books to be read aloud to them are often the very same people who believe that Santa Claus is real. As such, you should be sure to read aloud the first Author's Note on the preceding page and allow the listener to decide whether or not to go on with the rest.

The only other reason to move your mouth while reading would be if you were chewing gum or something, but this is not the sort of book that should be read while chewing gum.

# —— Third Author's Note ——

PLEASE REFRAIN FROM CHEWING GUM WHILE
reading this book.

# Preface

WHAT IS THE DIFFERENCE BETWEEN A PREFACE and an Author's Note? And where does the Introduction come into all of this? And why is there so much stuff you are required to get out of the way before the book gets started?

These are the questions that keep me up at night.

If you have an answer to one or more of them, please contact me at the address listed in the back of this book.

# Introduction

IF YOU HAVE NOT ALREADY READ THE THREE Author's Notes and the Preface, you may wish to go back and read them. They are brief, but they contain valuable information that could prevent you from harboring feelings of ill will toward me for the rest of your life (the information found in the first Author's Note is particularly helpful in this regard).

If you *have* read them, you will understand that I am not entirely sure of what is required before an author can go ahead and just start the book. I am putting this Introduction in place as a precautionary measure because you can never be too sure when it comes to the legalities of the publishing industry.

Thank you for your patience and understanding.

Now on to the good stuff!

# SECTION 2

## The Good Stuff

# 1

## — Telling Lies to Children —

STARTING A BOOK IS HARD.

I don't mean starting to read one, although sometimes that is tough too, especially if the print is very small or if it's in a language you don't know or you have a headache or someone is talking very loudly nearby.

But writing one is even harder. And the first sentence is particularly difficult because you've got to come up with something that will hook the reader right away, something catchy that will make them think, "Yeah, this guy is all right! I think I could spend a couple hundred pages with him!" Or if they're reading it on a Kindle, they will think, "Yeah, this guy is all right! I think I could spend a couple thousand locations with him!"

But either way, you've got to hook the reader right away.

For this reason, I thought about starting this book by saying, *"Hello, I'm Johnny Cash."*

Obviously I am not Johnny Cash because he is dead and I am not, and even when he was alive, I was not him.

But I want this book to sell a lot of copies, and it seems like things that start with *"Hello, I'm Johnny Cash"* sell a lot of copies.

My real name is Kyle Scheele, but that doesn't seem to have quite the same effect on people. I'm not exactly sure how many copies you sell when you start something with *"Hello, I'm Kyle Scheele"* because there aren't a lot of things that start that way. I'm actually not aware of any, to be honest with you. Perhaps my next book will start that way, and then I will be able to tell you how it affects sales. But for now I don't know.

In the end I decided against the Johnny Cash thing because it is probably not a great idea to start out a book by lying to the reader, at least not in a nonfiction book. Fiction books are okay to start with a lie because the whole thing is a lie. Fiction writers are just professional liars.

To tell you the truth, I am not a very good liar at all, which is probably why I have not published very many works of fiction. If I get better at lying in the future, I will consider getting into that market, but for now my lying skills are rather pathetic.

Whenever I try to lie to someone I start grinning like an idiot and trying not to laugh and it makes my face look very strange and then people know something is up. People that know me think I am a pretty honest guy, and I suppose it is true, but I don't know how much of that is just because I couldn't be a good liar if I wanted to.

My wife, on the other hand, is an excellent liar. If there were a competition for lying, I have no doubt she would be on the Olympic team. The only problem would be that people would see her dressed up in the stars and stripes and say, "Hey, wait a minute. Aren't you on the Olympic lying team?" and then they wouldn't believe anything she said, which would cause her to get very low scores. I think this is the main reason that lying is not an Olympic sport.

Don't get me wrong, I love my wife. And I don't think she is a pathological liar or anything. In fact, she is generally a very honest person. But when she wants to, she can convince people of things that are not true. Luckily, it's only a certain group of people, and I am not in that group anymore. I used to be, but that was a long time before I met her.

See, my wife likes to tell lies to small children, and I have not been a small child for some time now.

I found out about all of this when we were at the zoo a few years back. We were attempting to visit the monkeys, but things were not going quite as well as we had hoped. The problem was that the walking path only went along one side of the cage, and the monkeys were all on the opposite side.

I had hoped we would be able to see the monkeys up close, perhaps even shake hands with them through the bars of the cage and swap stories about how our lives were very different but in many ways the same. They would offer to share some of their food, which we would politely decline. But they would insist, so we would take a little and pretend to enjoy it, though secretly we would slip the rest into a napkin to be thrown away later. Eventually the zookeepers would tell us we had to leave because the zoo was closing, and we would tearfully part ways, having made new friends and learned a lot about ourselves.

But the monkeys were too far away for any of this. We could see them, but not very well, and it didn't seem like they had any interest in shaking hands anyway. It was disappointing, to be honest, but I couldn't really think of a way to remedy the situation. I figured we would just move on to another exhibit, perhaps the gorillas, which are a lot like monkeys but on a much larger scale.

But my wife was not about to give up so easily. She thought, "I came to this zoo to see monkeys, and I am not leaving this exhibit until I see some monkeys."

She didn't say this out loud, but I am pretty sure it was what she was thinking because out of nowhere she pointed and yelled, "Hey! You! Get over here!"

But she wasn't pointing and yelling at me. She was pointing and yelling at a monkey.

I don't know exactly what possessed her to do this, but I also don't know what possessed the monkey to listen to her, because he did. He just walked right over.

I realized in that moment that it is one thing to daydream about having a conversation with monkeys at the zoo and having them respond to you, and it is another thing entirely when it begins to actually happen in front of your eyes.

Before I could finish processing what had just occurred, I had the sudden realization that I was not the only one observing this situation. There was another family at the monkey cage, a mother and a father and a young girl who was probably seven or eight.

The mother and father had definitely seen what had happened, but they were old enough to know not to stare at anyone who is willing to scream at monkeys in public because you may accidentally make eye contact and then who knows what sort of danger you would be in?

But the little girl was too young to know any of this, so she was staring at my wife with her mouth wide open and a look on her face that said, *"Oh my word... this woman can talk to animals."*

My wife had not seen the girl because she was still locked in a fierce staring contest with the monkey. I broke her concentration and whispered, "Babe. Look over there."

My wife glanced over at the girl and immediately knew what was going on. Anyone who saw the girl's face would've known. Her gaping mouth was silent, but her expression clearly said, *"Who is this woman? Even the monkeys obey her!"*

My wife walked over to the girl, leaning down and putting her hand on the child's shoulder as if to tell her that there was a perfectly good explanation for all of this. At least, that's what I thought she was going to tell her. Instead, she said this:

"You know, a lot of people won't tell you this because you're a kid, but since you paid money to get into the zoo..."

She paused, glancing left and right to make sure no one was listening, then whispered,

*".... the monkeys have to do whatever you tell them."*

She stood up straight, gave the girl a pat on the shoulder, then briskly walked away, leaving me standing alone.

I caught up to my wife at the elephant enclosure, where she luckily had not found it necessary to scream at the animals yet.

"Hey...um...babe?" I said.

"Yes, sweetheart?" she said, as if nothing out of the ordinary had just occurred.

"Well, I was just wondering... What exactly happened back there?" I said.

"Oh, that!" she said, laughing a little. "I forgot to tell you this, but I love telling lies to little kids. They'll believe *anything* you tell them!"

I learned a lot about my wife that day.

But since then I have learned an even more disturbing fact: my wife is not the only person who enjoys telling lies to children. Far from it. In fact, the vast majority of adults lie to kids all the time. That's actually the number one thing about being an adult: learning to tell convincing lies to children. This, among other things, may be the reason I am not considered a very good adult.

You might think I'm exaggerating, that things can't possibly be as bad as I am making them out to be. But you would be wrong, and I can prove it to you. In fact, I can prove it with just two words. These two words sum up the greatest lie ever told to children, a lie that spans across continents and generations, a lie that has been used to deceive billions and billions of children around the world for centuries.

Two words: *Santa. Claus.*

Santa Claus is not only the biggest and most successful lie ever told to children, it is also the most confusing. I don't understand the point of it.

Here's what I mean: as a parent, I love buying things for my kids. When I buy my kids something, it is my way of saying, "I worked hard and earned money, but instead of spending it on myself, I want to show you how much you mean to me by buying you something that you want."

But the Santa Claus lie doesn't allow me to say that. Instead I have to say, "I bet you're wondering where these presents came from. Well, let me tell you. There's this big, creepy old man who *looooves* kids. And once a year, he breaks into your house. You can't stop him, either. You can lock the doors and bolt the windows, but he's getting in. And once he's inside, he leaves you presents, things you've been hoping and wishing for."

"But how does he know what I want?" the kids ask.

So we tell them, *"He's been watching you while you sleep."*

This is a story we tell to children.

So like I said, I don't understand the Santa Claus thing. But I do understand this: I have to be careful about talking about it, about exposing the truth that Santa is not, in fact, *a real person.*

I know this because of an experience I had a few years ago.

I was speaking to a group of teenagers in California, mostly junior high and high school students. I was talking about how sometimes in life you will learn a simple fact, something that really isn't significant to other people, but this one fact somehow flips your entire world on its head.

As an example, I said, "I remember the day that I found out Santa Claus isn't real."

At the time, I thought the only people in the group were junior high and high school students. I soon found out I was mistaken, that there was also a small contingency of fifth graders present, sitting in the back corner.

I think you can see where this is going.

So I said, "I remember the day I found out Santa Claus isn't real." And no sooner had the words left my lips than this little fifth-grade girl in the very back of the room said,

*"He's NOT?!?!"*

She then proceeded to burst into tears.

In the script for the talk, I had planned on saying something like, "Everyone is pretending like they knew already, but there are probably a few kids crying in the back corner because they didn't know..." Which is a funny joke when you are in a room full of people who already knew that Santa Claus is not real.

It turned out I was not in such a room.

As such, I had to quickly skip over that line because there actually *was* someone crying in the back corner. For the next 25 minutes.

That was a traumatic experience for both of us. For her because her entire childhood came crumbling down around her in a shower of broken dreams right in front of her friends, and for me because I was worried that I was going to get an angry letter from her parents and never be asked to speak to that group again.

All of that to say, I understand why people tell lies to children. It's much easier that way and involves significantly less crying, at least in my experience.

The girl at the zoo didn't cry at all when my wife told her she could order the monkeys around like servants, although perhaps she cried later when she found out it wasn't true. But at least we weren't around to see it when it happened.

# 2

## Everything You Know is Wrong

I GUESS WHAT I AM TRYING TO SAY HERE IS that if you are under a certain age, it is quite likely that just about everything you know about the world is completely untrue, or at least mostly untrue.

Don't feel bad though. That's part of life. We've all believed things that later turned out to be totally wrong.

Sometimes these things don't really matter that much, like if you believe Santa Claus is bringing you presents when it is really your parents. You are going to get the presents either way, so your belief about where they came from doesn't really change anything — unless you are a particular fifth grader in California and a guy named Kyle comes to speak to a group of your friends. In that case, you may end up with deep emotional scars that require years of counseling to work out.

But other times these things matter more, like when you believe it is okay to go without deodorant even when the people around you are giving you *very clear signals* that it is not. Seriously, Bill. Is it a money thing? I told you, we are all willing to chip in a few bucks.

The point is, you shouldn't be ashamed to find out you've believed things that aren't true. You should only be ashamed if you continue to believe those things.

Personally, I've believed all sorts of untrue things over the years. Most of them have been things that really didn't change my life in any way, like when I asked someone how they were doing and they said, "Fine." and I believed them, even though they were *really* feeling a sense of regret over eating shrimp tacos from a fast food place. But I've also believed other lies, more substantial ones, things with pretty serious consequences.

The worst lies I've believed have all had to do with the big questions of how the world works and what people should do with their lives. Those are bad things to get wrong, certainly much more consequential than beliefs about deodorant or Santa Claus. But I'm not the only one who has messed this stuff up. I think a lot of us get this wrong, actually. But can you blame us? From the moment we're born we are constantly getting conflicting messages about what life is and what it can be.

When you are young, you're told, "You can be whatever you want to be when you grow up!" So you dream of being an astronaut or a firefighter or a ballerina. You dream of being elected president and giving everyone in the country free candy and flying puppies.

But then you get older and you hear, "You can do anything you *set your mind to.*"

This means you can still do whatever you want, but only if you *set your mind to it.* But what does that even mean?

How do you *set your mind* to something? Do you just think about it really hard? Or put your brain really close to the thing, pressing it to your forehead and squinting your eyes to concentrate the brain waves?

You don't really have time to figure out how it's done though, because the "You can do anything you set your mind to" phase doesn't last long. Pretty soon the message starts to change again, and the same people who said you could be an astronaut or a ballerina begin saying things like, "You know, that's a hard career to get into..." and "Maybe you should think about a backup plan."

Before you know it they are giving you suggestions of other things you could do, jobs where you could make more money, careers with more stability or prestige. Then suddenly the backup plan becomes the only plan, and people who are still pursuing the things they wanted all along are written off as crazy dreamers with unrealistic expectations of life.

Obviously not all adults are like this. Plenty of adults encourage young people to keep following their dreams even when those dreams are tough or unrealistic by everyone else's standards. Plenty of parents encourage their sons and daughters to try new things, to seek out new experiences and learn new skills.

But oftentimes those encouraging voices can be drowned out by the discouraging ones. Sometimes the crowd of adults telling young people to "be realistic" will even criticize the adults who are encouraging them to pursue their dreams, saying they are setting the kids up for disappointment, that the real world doesn't work the way they are pretending it does.

Is it any wonder we end up confused about this stuff, that we wind up believing things that aren't true? With all of the mixed messages and conflicting advice, is it any wonder that we can't seem to figure out what we are supposed to do with our lives?

When I was a kid, I wrote a letter to Robert Ballard, the guy who found *the Titanic* after it had been on the bottom of the ocean for 73 years.

I was supposed to be writing a report about the mountains on the ocean floor or something, and Robert Ballard was technically a marine geologist. But he seemed more like a treasure hunter to me, and that's what I really wanted to write about, so I found his address in the library and mailed him a letter. He wrote back thanking me for my interest in his work and giving me an update on what he was working on. He even sent some pictures of himself in a tiny submarine.

I'm sure it was a form letter, the same one he sent to a million other kids. But it had a huge impact on me because it arrived right around the time people were starting to talk about backup plans and having realistic expectations in life and all of that. And right in the middle of it all comes this letter from a guy who searches for shipwrecks for a living.

I remember taking the letter to school and showing it to all of my friends, trying to act as though Robert Ballard and I were old pals, like he might take me on his next trip down to the Titanic, might let me bring back a piece of treasure from the ship if I behaved myself.

I kept that letter for years and years, even after I figured out that it was probably sent by an assistant, some poor college intern who answered the mail while Robert Ballard was out to sea. I didn't even read it anymore, but I kept it on a shelf inside a manila envelope on which my mother had written "Kyle's Letter from Bob Ballard".

It wasn't anything about what was written in the letter itself that kept me from getting rid of it. It was the simple fact that this guy had a completely unreasonable career, one without room for backup plans or playing it safe. And this letter was like a relic, something that came from him (or at least from his address), something that proved it was possible to do what you love, to have the sort of job you dreamed about as a kid.

That letter was my glimmer of hope, the one sign that just *maybe* I didn't have to settle.

For the record, I understand why adults start talking about backup plans and career stability. The vast majority of these people really do think they have your best interests at heart. They don't want you to be starving and broke in your thirties and forties. And if they are your parents, they also don't want to have to keep paying your bills forever, which is understandable.

But the danger comes when we reduce life to nothing more than dollars and cents, when every decision is determined based on financial cost. Obviously bills need to be paid and we should all be responsible enough to cover our own expenses, but I think we get into trouble when we start pretending money is everything.

I once knew a girl whose parents were self-made millionaires. And when I say self-made, I mean it. They started with *nothing.* I remember hearing them tell stories about the early days of their married life, how they would run out of grocery money at the end of the month and have to eat microwave popcorn for dinner. They told me how they once put their infant daughter inside the clothes dryer during a tornado because they lived in a trailer and that was the safest place they could think of.

I remember after hearing these stories, I said to my friend's mom, "Man, that sounds terrible..."

And she said, "Terrible? It was *wonderful.* Those were some of the best times of our lives."

They weren't one of those couples who had been driven apart by the money or anything like that, either. They were very happily married. But she told me that when they were poor, all they had was each other. All they had were the memories they were making, the stories of how they made it through. And years later, when they had millions of dollars and a giant house on 200 acres of land, the things that mattered most were their stories.

I remember getting the feeling from these people that the money wasn't really that important. Yes, it allowed them to have some nice things, and it certainly made life a little easier in some ways, but it was not the all-consuming passion that money becomes for most people. It was just another thing. And if they had lost it all, I think their lives would have gone on in much the same way.

In fact, aside from the house and the land, you would never even know that these people were rich. They didn't wear expensive clothes or drive fancy cars or any of that.

They weren't flashy with their money, which is probably why they were able to keep so much of it around. They were incredibly generous, too. If I had to guess, they probably spent more money helping the people around them than they did on themselves.

I have known lots of people with money in my life, and it seems as though the ones who were happiest were the ones who cared about it the least, who weren't constantly clawing for more. It's the people who realized they may not be rich forever, that they should use their money to help other people while they can.

It's sad to me, then, that we spend so much of our time worrying about this thing that is neither good nor bad in and of itself, that can do as much damage as it can bring benefit. In the wrong hands, money brings nothing but heartache and pain. It divides families and turns children rotten. It is consistently one of the leading causes of divorce.

And yet, it's often what we steer our children towards.

*Don't be an artist, you won't make any money that way.*

*Don't get into theater, there's no money in that.*

*Don't be a writer, you'll be poor all your life.*

But will you be happy? Will you live with excitement because you love what you do? Then I say you should do it.

I have never met a person who was happy and excited about his work and simultaneously full of regret over the way his life had turned out. On the other hand, I have met *plenty* of people who pursued wealth and safety at the cost of their dreams, only to end up with riches and comfort and a consuming emptiness inside.

I once heard someone say there is nothing we own that isn't 50 years away from a landfill. But I don't think that's accurate. I think if we're honest, most of our stuff is probably only 10 years away from being garbage, at best. The things that are important to us now will be forgotten as quickly as they came, replaced by something newer and shinier and with an even shorter shelf life. But the things we have done, the memories we have made, the experiences we have had with the people we love... those things will live on.

The stories we live will be the only things that last, the only things that matter. Long after the money and houses and trinkets are gone, our stories will be the things that determine whether our lives were well-lived or wasted.

Our stories will define us.

# 3

## — We Put a Man on the Moon —

MY FRIEND MATT IS A LIAR, BUT HE MEANS WELL.

If Matt thinks of something that would make a good story, he will tell it to you like it is true, like it really happened to him. Then once you have had time to enjoy the story, he will let you know he made the whole thing up.

He is the most honest liar I know.

Once Matt and I were driving through Kansas City, where he lives. I had never spent much time there before so he was pointing out various landmarks as we drove around town.

As we passed a particularly high bridge, Matt pointed his finger.

"See that?" he said. "They call that Dead Man's Bridge."

"Oh yeah?" I said. "How come?"

"People are always trying to dive off of it, but the water isn't deep enough. They have to put cops around it all the time to keep people from jumping off and accidentally killing themselves. Every year about fifty people die there."

"That's crazy." I said.

That night I was getting ready to go to bed in the guest room at Matt's parents' house. He showed me where everything was, then he turned to head back to his own room.

"Goodnight, Kyle." he said.

"Goodnight, Matt." I said back.

"Oh, Kyle?" he said.

"Yeah, Matt?" I said.

"I made up that whole story about Dead Man's Bridge. I don't know why. It just seemed like the kind of thing that might be true, and I figured it would sound dumb if I said 'Wouldn't it be weird if they called that Dead Man's Bridge because people jumped off it all the time or something but the water wasn't deep enough?' I figured if I said that, you'd probably think I was a weirdo. So instead, I just told it like it was true. Anyways, I just wanted you to know I made it up. I didn't want to lie to you." he said

"Good to know, man." I said back.

"Oh, and Matt?" I said

"Yeah, Kyle?" said Matt.

"You're a weirdo." I said.

Matt had good intentions, but I've known other people who lived their whole lives like that and never came clean about it.

One summer I was working as a counselor at a YMCA Camp. One of the other counselors, a guy named Ryan, was always telling the craziest stories about his life and all of the cool things he had done. He was very popular because he always had the best stories.

Once, Ryan was telling us about how his girlfriend missed him while he was gone working at camp.

"She doesn't feel safe knowing I'm so far away," he said, "So I took a picture of myself with a Polaroid camera and stuck the picture to her pillow. So now she feels like I'm always there."

All the girls swooned. You could almost hear their hearts pitter-pattering for this guy.

That weekend I went home for a few days. While I was there, I happened to turn on the television while I was waiting for a load of laundry to finish drying.

The first thing that came on was a Polaroid commercial. In the commercial, this guy was going on a trip and he had to leave early in the morning while the rest of his family was still sleeping. Before he left though, he took a picture of himself and stuck the Polaroid to his pillow so that his wife would see it when she woke up.

What a coincidence!

As the summer went on, more and more of Ryan's stories turned out to be untrue. Many of them were taken directly from television or the movies. It was almost as if Ryan was counting on the fact that none of us watched TV since we were gone at camp all summer.

By the end of the summer, nobody listened to anything Ryan had to say anymore. We couldn't tell where Ryan's real life ended and his deception began. To this day I am not sure if Ryan even *had* a girlfriend, or if he simply made one up so he could tell that story.

The saddest thing of all was that Ryan could not seem to

tell either. He had been lying to so many people for so long that I don't even think *he* knew what was true anymore.

I understand why Ryan would want to live like that though, why he would feel the need to make his life seem better than it actually is.

Living good stories is hard. Actually having an interesting life, the kind of life that good stories come out of, takes a lot of work. It means you've gotta get out of bed and do a lot of interesting things instead of watching TV or eating popcorn or checking your Facebook again and again and again and again.

In the town where I live, there is a girl named Elsie who runs a very successful blog about fashion and craft projects and other cool stuff. Last month she had over a hundred thousand visitors to her site.

I know this because over the last few months it seems like everyone I know has mentioned this girl to me. They talk about how she is such a great blogger, how her projects are so cool, her story so inspiring.

And all of that is true. She has done something really incredible, building a loyal following of thousands and thousands of people with just a computer and a camera and a lot of hard work.

But I started poking around her site and asking questions of people who know her, trying to find out a little bit more about her story. And it turns out she has been doing this for over five years. Half a decade! And it's only been in the past six months or so that I have started hearing about her all the time.

That means she was working for *years* before I ever heard of her, before everyone I know started talking about her. Obviously I am not the measure of whether or not someone is famous, but the point remains that this girl had a dream and worked at it for a very long time before it turned into something big.

I guarantee you there were times along the way when it got tough, times when she was juggling the blog and all of her other commitments, times when she wasn't getting as many visitors to the site as she would like. I bet there were times when she was tempted to throw in the towel, to give it all up and settle for something easier. But she didn't. She kept at it, and little by little she turned it into the thing she had been aiming for all along.

Living good stories is like that. It takes a lot of hard work for a really long time. And even then, there is no guarantee that it will work out. You could fall flat on your face and fail miserably. And who wants to do that? It is much easier to just make something up and pretend it is true, like it really happened to you. It is much easier to borrow someone else's story and pretend it is your own.

Sometimes I worry about my generation and the ones to follow. I worry that we have so much great stuff, so much incredible technology and such an amazing quality of life that we have become content just to take it all in.

I am worried we have become consumers rather than producers.

I am worried we are all going to have the same stories to tell at the end of our lives, stories about watching cats do funny things on the internet, about playing video games, about television shows and funny commercials.

I am worried we will never venture out to do amazing things, see incredible places, overcome overwhelming adversity.

Several decades ago, right as TV was getting popular, when the price of a television set came down to where everyone could afford one, the United States put a man on the moon.

We put a *human being* inside a rocket, lit the fuse, shot him into space, and then he walked around on the moon, bouncing up in the air and then slowly floating back down again. He took some pictures and collected some rocks and stuck a flag in the ground in case somebody else came by and wondered who left their spaceship there.

But then once he got back, I think everyone started telling him about all of the great shows he missed while he was gone, because he never went back after that. And pretty soon we stopped sending people altogether. We didn't even go back to get the flag. We stopped exploring cool places and instead started sending robots to space so we could watch their adventures on a screen while we flipped between the other channels.

These days most of the rockets going into space are carrying satellites so we can get better cell phone reception or a clearer signal for our TV. And there's a little part of me that is very sad about that. There's a part of me that wishes we didn't have all of the great stuff we have now because maybe then we would have more incentive to live better stories. Nowadays we only go outside when there is nothing good on TV, but TV shows are getting better all the time so pretty soon we might not go outside at all.

Soon we will take in all of our adventures vicariously through a screen, like fluids through an IV. Our children will see footage of the space program on the internet and ask, "Is this real? Is it true? We put a man on the moon?"

And we will say, "Yes, it is true. We put a man on the moon. But that was a long time ago, and those were different times."

We will pause, shaking our head slowly from side to side.

*"Those were very different times."* we will say again, for emphasis.

Then we will turn back to our phone or computer, putting on headphones to signal that we are no longer taking questions. We will settle back into our comfortable chairs and bask in the warm glow of a digital screen, drawn in like moths to a flame.

# 4

## —— Cheating for Idiots ——

THIS FUTURE IS INEVITABLE BECAUSE OF ONE simple fact: most people go for what is easy in life. They take the path of least resistance.

It is easy to copy other people's stories, easy to go along with what everyone else is doing. It is easy to accept the status quo.

The problem is that great things are rarely easy and easy things are rarely great. For example, dunking on a six-foot basketball goal: It's fun and it makes you feel like an athlete for a moment, but it doesn't impress anyone who is over the age of eight.

And more importantly, it doesn't make you an athlete. It makes you a wannabe, a hack, a fraud.

I am an inch or two over six feet tall, so it is not inconceivable that I could dunk a basketball if I wanted to. But I would have to lose some weight and practice jumping a lot and probably do some squats or a whole bunch of lunges or something to build up my leg muscles. And that frankly sounds like a lot of work when I could just lower the rim a few feet and then go back to my regular life.

Living a better story is like that, too. It sounds really great until you realize how hard it is going to be. And then you look at TV and the movies and your friends' lives and realize there are plenty of good stories already out there, so why not just copy one of those?

I'm a youth speaker, and sometimes when I am talking to an audience of teenagers I will say that I am going to tell them a little bit about myself, about my life story. Then I'll say something like, "When I was a kid, my parents were brutally murdered, right in front of my eyes...."

There is always an audible gasp from the crowd at this point, so I will pause for a second as if I'm about to cry and need to collect myself. Then I take a deep breath and say, ".....by an evil wizard named Lord Voldemort."

But the thing is, I take longer than that to tell it, adding in details about how young I was, how I was barely old enough to remember it, how I was powerless to do anything. I load the whole story up with details so anyone listening would believe I was actually there. Then at the very end, I say the line about Lord Voldemort and everybody realizes I was lying.

People laugh though because it is kind of fun to be tricked every now and then.

Then I will say, "Okay, okay, I was obviously joking. But here's my real story: My parents really *were* murdered in front of my eyes, but I wasn't a baby. I was older, and we were at a movie theater. Afterwards, we stepped out into the alley beside the theater. My parents were a ways ahead of me when suddenly a man stepped out of the shadows, pulled out a gun and demanded that my parents give him their money. He was pointing the gun right at my mom, so my dad stepped in front to protect her. The man thought my dad was trying to take the gun or something so he pulled the trigger, killing my father. Then he shot my mother and ran away."

As this point, the audience is usually pretty quiet. Some of the girls look like they might start crying a little. So I only pause for a second before I say, "And that was when I vowed to stop the crime in Gotham City. That's when I decided to become... the Batman."

That usually gets a laugh, but then it gets quiet again. After this second lie, people realize I am not being honest, and they start to wonder if I am doing this to make a point or if I am just some kind of deranged lunatic, some sort of pathologically dishonest youth speaker. And then they wonder who signed off on letting me come speak to their school.

But that's when I swoop in and alleviate their fears. I tell them I am obviously lying, but I was doing it to make a point. I was doing it to show how absurd it is. And they think *well of course it's absurd.*

And then I say "...but it's just as absurd when you do it."

Perhaps it's a bit melodramatic, but it gets the point across. See, so many times we can look at other people's lives and criticize some aspect of their behavior, not realizing that all the while we are doing the same thing on a smaller scale or in a different way.

It is easy for me to look at Ryan's life and think it is pathetic that he copies Polaroid commercials, but is it any less pathetic when I try to live a story that is based on popular opinion or the status quo instead of being based on my gifts, my talents, my interests and skills?

If I'm honest, it's not. If anything, it is probably *more* pathetic. At least Ryan is copying stories that move us, stories that provoke an emotional response. At least Ryan is copying stories that are good, stories crafted by advertisers and screenwriters to make us feel certain things.

Me, on the other hand? Oftentimes I am copying stories that, if I'm honest, are not about anything moving at all. They are boring stories about playing it safe and not sticking my neck out too far, stories about staying in line and doing what I am told, about coloring inside the lines and only with the set of crayons I have been given.

In the end, is that really any different than stealing scenes from movies and commercials?

I don't think it is.

Since I am a motivational youth speaker, people always think I am into cheesy sayings and posters with kittens on them. But I'm not. I hate that stuff. And I think that most of those sayings are blatantly untrue.

But some of them aren't.

Like the whole "You are unique, a one-of-a-kind snowflake!" thing. To be honest, I still don't entirely believe that every snowflake is different. How could they possibly know that?

But you *are* unique. You *are* one-of-a-kind. Just look at your DNA. There has never been anybody with exactly the same genes, exactly the same experiences, exactly the same life as you. If there was, you would be running into them all the time and wondering why they keep following you into the bathroom.

But since that isn't happening to you (and if it is, then frankly you have bigger issues than I am qualified to address), it means you are not just a carbon copy of somebody else.

Now by itself, that is not really saying much. We have all known some weirdos who were certainly very "unique", to say the least. But in terms of shaping your story, this idea is a powerful one because your uniqueness means you weren't given the same materials everyone else was given to build their stories. You were given a different set. So it doesn't make sense to try and build another person's story because you don't have the right supplies.

Or to put it another way: the *Star Wars* movies are great, but people who live like *Star Wars* is *real*... are weird.

Have you seen these people? There are people out there who go to conventions to talk about *Star Wars*, and they dress up in Stormtrooper gear and play role-playing games and build fake lightsabers and stuff. Frankly, their behavior is more than a little concerning.

I am all for having fun, and there is nothing wrong with having a costume party or playing a game sometimes. But when it gets to the point where your fake life is better than your real life, you are probably using the game to escape something.

I read an article the other day about a guy who had spent *thousands of dollars* to build a custom replica of the armor suit worn by the guy in the *HALO* video games.

That is ridiculous.

My first thought was, "Somebody should shoot this guy."

Not to kill him, but just to show him that his armor

doesn't work. Because if he realizes that, maybe he'll see how dumb it is to wear it all the time. Or ever.

See, it makes sense for the guy in the *HALO* game to wear armor. Because in his story, the armor protects him. And in his story, people are shooting at him all the time. So he needs all of that.

But if you are a mid-level accountant, you don't need body armor. Especially *costume* body armor that probably wouldn't stop a paintball.

So many of us live our lives exactly like this, just in more subtle ways. We play sports we have no interest in because somebody tells us we should. We buy clothes we don't like to fit in with people who don't really care about us. We spend time and money and emotional energy acquiring things that make no sense in the context of our stories.

When you think about it, is that really any more ridiculous than stealing your stories from a commercial? I don't think so.

When I was in high school, I was a year ahead of my class in mathematics. I'd gone to a different middle school and taken a different set of classes, so when I got to high school I found out I was a little bit ahead in a few subjects.

So while the rest of the people my age were taking Algebra I, I was taking Algebra II.

I was also involved in a lot of extracurriculars in high school. I was on a few sports teams, in several clubs, on a handful of committees... so it was not unusual for me to miss class in order to attend an event or a competition or a game or something.

On one particular occasion, I missed my Algebra II class on the day of a test. I had let the teacher know about it in advance though, so she said I could come back another time to make it up.

We looked at our schedules and found another time for me to come back, a time that would work for me without disrupting any of her classes. It just so happened we were able to find another one of her classes that was taking a test I could sit in on.

The only thing was, this was an Algebra I class.

It didn't really matter of course, because she gave me the Algebra II test. I was only there because it was a quiet room and I wasn't going to be a distraction to anyone else.

But the kid next to me did not know I was taking an Algebra II test. At least, I don't think he knew because as soon as the test started he began copying my answers.

At first I didn't know what to do. On one hand, I was not a person who let people copy my tests, because I didn't want teachers to think I was participating in any kind of cheating. I also thought it was unfair that someone else would take advantage of the time I had spent studying.

But in this case, I was willing to make an exception. I looked up at the teacher, who was watching the whole thing. I shot her a look that said, "What do I do?"

She just winked and gave me a thumbs up.

So I let him cheat. And he cheated. He copied every single answer on my entire test.

Every. Single. One.

When we got the tests back, I got an A on mine. I don't

think he did so well on his, though.

He came up me in the hall a few days later and said, "Dude, I thought you were smart!"

I wanted to say, "Really? I never thought that about you..."

In a way, this is what stealing stories is like. It's like copying answers to the wrong test.

Because we're all unique, right? So for each of us, the test becomes "Will you live the stories you were designed to live? Will you put your unique set of life circumstances to use to build the greatest possible story?"

If you are trying to use your material to take the test of the kid next to you, you are going to fail. The story you build will not work, and you will be leaving all of your best materials — your skills, talents, passions, interests — on the table.

Like it or not, you are playing with a different set of cards than the kid next to you. And they are not even the same *kind* of cards. He might have a royal flush and you've got a set of Uno cards.

Or greeting cards. Or baseball cards. Or credit cards.

Who knows? But the point is, you are playing a totally different game. You are building a totally different story. So why copy his strategy? Why peek at his hand? It's of no consequence to you. Just worry about playing the hand you've got and let him worry about his. In the end, that's all you can do. But it's enough for a great story.

You know why it's enough? Because it's not a competition. Life is one of the only games where more than one person can win. Your neighbor living an incredible story won't keep you from living one just as good. *Unless* you try to steal his formula. That's the only way to guarantee that you lose: try and be something you're not.

As much as I hate to say anything that remotely sounds like it could be on a poster with a kitten, the fact is that you are unique. You are one-of-a-kind. And with that uniqueness comes a responsibility to use the materials you were given to tell the story you were meant to tell.

# 5

## — No More Good Choices —

HOW COME WE DON'T TALK ABOUT THIS STUFF in school? How come we rarely hear adults telling us to live better stories?

I don't know the answer because I am not usually seen as a productive member of the adult world, so I am not invited to the secret meetings where they make these decisions. But I have a few guesses.

I think the main reason we don't talk about this stuff is because it is tough to mass-produce. It is not one-size-fits-all. Each person's story has to be custom tailored for that person, or else you end up with an accountant walking around in four thousand dollars worth of *HALO* armor.

The idea of custom-building good stories for millions and millions of people is overwhelming. So instead we talk about things that *can* be mass-produced, things like *success* and *making good choices*. We say, "If you make good choices, you'll be successful!"

I always thought this was a strange tactic. People like to use the "make good choices" thing as a motivator, putting up cheesy kitten posters praising the idea of positive choice. But it's not really all that motivating. When you think about it, it's just someone else telling me what to do with my life.

It's easier to talk about though because it's one-size-fits-all. Anyone can do it. In fact, I don't even have to *know you* to tell you how to be successful.

I'll just plug you into a formula:

- Get *this kind* of GPA.

- Do *these kinds* of extracurriculars.

- Go to *this kind* of college.

- Take *these kinds* of classes.

- Get *this kind* of degree.

- Land *this kind* of internship, which leads to *this kind* of job making *this kind* of money.

- Marry *this kind* of person and have *this kind* of kid.

- Buy *this kind* of house in *this kind* of neighborhood.

- Drive *this kind* of car.

It's easy! Plug anybody into that equation, have them complete all the steps, and SHAZAM! Success!

Funny though, isn't it? We tell you exactly what to do, exactly where to go, exactly how to live your life so that you never have to think, and then what do we call the process? *Making choices.*

Sounds to me like the choices have already been made.

The problem with this whole thing, aside from the blatant misuse of the word "choice", is that it is not true. It doesn't work.

The idea that "if you make good choices, you will be successful" sounds so good on the surface, and part of me desperately wants it to be true because then it puts everything in my grasp.

*I am in control! My success or failure depends solely on me!*

But that isn't accurate, is it? I mean, in your experience, has that proven to be true? It hasn't in mine.

A lot of this depends on how you define things like good choices and bad choices, success and failure. But I think for most of us, a big part of the idea of success is tied to material wealth. If you are rich, you are successful. If you have money and houses and cars and a swimming pool full of gold coins, you are successful. If you are poor and have no job and have a hard time paying your bills, you're unsuccessful.

You might think this is not true for you, that you are not so shallow. You might think that your definition of success is not so narrow. But you are not being honest with yourself. Think of the first three people that come to your mind when you think of the word "success". Are any of them poor? Do any of them have a hard time making ends meet?

Probably not. As much as we would like to think otherwise, a big part of success for us is tied to our bank account.

Then we define bad choices as abusing alcohol and drugs, having unprotected sex, that sort of thing. And we define good choices simply as "staying away from bad choices."

That's probably the worst part of all: our standards have fallen so far that to be considered "good" all you really have to be is "not bad".

This is the roadmap we use for making choices and finding success. But I think if we're honest, we know these things are not inherently linked together. Good choices don't guarantee success, and bad choices don't guarantee failure.

I have known plenty of people who have made great choices, who have done all the right things, but who have ultimately ended up getting punched in the gut by life, left doubled over and sputtering for air.

I have known people who worked very hard for a long time, who worked long hours at a difficult job to support their families, who sacrificed and worked hard to move up in the company, and then one day the boss said, "Well, it's been a good run, buddy. See you later!" and the whole company packed up and left town.

I have known people who lost their jobs when the economy turned bad, or the company moved out of state, or out of the country, or went out of business altogether.

Not because of any choices they made, not because of anything they did wrong.

I have known people who worked for years and years to pay off their houses, only to watch them be demolished by a tornado or a hurricane. I have known people who made all the right choices, did all the right things, checked all the right boxes, only to find out they had terminal cancer and wouldn't live to see the fruit of their hard work.

These things had nothing to do with the choices these people made. There is nothing you can *choose* that will keep bad things from happening to you. The whole "good choices = success" thing is a fundamentally broken equation.

This is not the kind of thing I am supposed to tell people about as a motivational speaker, but it is true. This stuff happens every day.

But that's not even the worst part. The worst part is when the opposite happens, when people make terrible choices, squander every resource and opportunity given to them, and somehow end up wildly successful. And this happens *all the time,* too.

It happens so much that we came up with a word for these people: *Celebrities.*

I can't be a hundred percent certain since I am not one, but I'm pretty sure that when you become a celebrity, you sign a contract with the general public that says, "You give me lots of money and attention, and I will let you watch my train wreck of a life unfold on national television."

I haven't seen the contract or anything, but how could it not be true? Turn on the television for five seconds and you can see it for yourself.

Obviously I am not saying that all celebrities are bad, because there are a lot of famous people who do a lot of really great things for the world.

But there are also a great number of people who are rich and famous and have no good stories to tell for it, no shred of evidence of a life well-lived. They spend their days numbing the pain with alcohol and drugs and scores of other bad decisions. But in the end, they still have more money, power, and fame than you and I will ever have.

How is that fair?

It's not fair. But it's true.

There are lots and lots of people out there who make horrible decisions, squander all of their potential, throw away every advantage life gives them, and somehow still manage to come out on top.

This is more than a little depressing when you think about it. Remember that whole "life isn't fair" thing your parents were always saying? Turns out they were right. In the worst possible way.

But if you think about it, is that what you want anyway? Riches and fame at the cost of squandered potential? At the cost of ruined relationships and a life full of regret? Is success worth that price?

If someone came to you and said, "Let me make you an offer. I will give you so much money that you will not know how to spend it. You will have houses and cars and fine clothes, exotic foods and a staff of servants to follow your every command. You will have everything you could ever imagine. And you will be *famous!* When you are at a restaurant, people will whisper at the tables next to you, saying, 'Look, it's him!' They will ask for your autograph and want to take pictures, saying they are your biggest fans. Everywhere you go, crowds of adoring followers will go crazy with excitement."

"In exchange, all I ask is that you give me all meaning and joy from your life. You will have everything you want on the outside, but inside you will be hollow and dead. You will never hunger for food, but you will cry yourself to sleep at night from the gnawing feeling of hopelessness that you feel."

Would you take that deal?

I doubt it. But so many people do.

See, it is entirely possible to get to the end of your life and be wildly successful and completely hollow inside.

It is possible to be rich and famous, with a garage full of cars and a house big enough to build another house inside, and yet ultimately have nothing to show for your life. No one who loves you, no one who cares about you, no one who would be there for you if your success was pulled out from under your feet.

No meaning. No purpose. No sign that you've made any sort of difference in this world.

You're just a guy with a lot of money, and the world will forget you the moment you're gone. To me, that's just not worth much of anything.

That's not the kind of life I want to live.

If that is success, then count me out.

# 6

# — Prank Calling the President —

WHEN I WAS IN HIGH SCHOOL, MY CHURCH youth group had a Christmas party. It was a Sunday night and we had all gathered in a coffee shop for a laid-back evening, for some fun and games and a celebration of the semester being over.

One of the games was an eggnog drinking contest. This was obviously non-alcoholic eggnog, but that doesn't mean that it wasn't still a terrible, terrible idea.

Somehow I managed to be chosen for the competition and I found myself on a stage with three other kids from the youth group, two girls and a guy. The leader in charge of the game told us we would be playing for a prize, but we wouldn't find out what the prize was until after the game was over.

Instead, he had us turn and face the back of the stage while he showed the prize to the people behind us in the audience. Based on their reaction, we had to judge whether or not we thought the prize was cool. And based on that, we would judge how badly we wanted to win the eggnog drinking competition.

The guy (His name was Sam. Actually, his name is still Sam.) held up the prize, and the crowd cheered and clapped. It was apparently something good.

Now I like eggnog, but it is a very rich drink. You really shouldn't have more than a cup or so at a time. For one thing there are about a billion calories in it, but more importantly, you will start to feel sick if you drink any more than that. It is just a very rich drink, thick like melted ice cream or the yolks of raw eggs.

That night I had seven cups of it. And not little cups, either. We're talking about those big red plastic party cups.

Seven of them.

And since it was a timed competition I drank those seven cups in under four minutes. I was drinking that eggnog like my life depended on it.

I won the competition, and Sam went over and brought me my prize. It was one of those huge Christmas tins full of different kinds of stale popcorn.

I had been duped.

Almost as soon as I walked off the stage, I began to think, "That may have been a bad decision..." as my stomach began to rumble.

I set the popcorn tin in my seat and told my friends not to open it. I figured I could at least regift it to someone else so it would not be a total loss.

Then I went into the bathroom and threw up seven cups of eggnog.

When I got back, my friend Nathan said, "You don't look so good, man. Your face looks all flushed." But it came out like "Yodunlutsogutman...yafalukalfluh" because he said it with fistfuls of stale cheesy popcorn in his mouth.

Fistfuls of *my* stale cheesy popcorn...

I imagine this is what it's like for people who spend their whole lives chasing money and success. They work so hard to win, and then they get the prize and think, "*This* is what I was working for?"

That's the thing about money. Nobody gets to the end of life and really cares very much about it. It's nice to have, and it certainly enables you to do certain things that would have otherwise been difficult, but it's not a necessity.

In the end, you can't take any of it with you. When you are 95 years old, hooked up to oxygen in your hospital bed, is it really going to matter how many Porsches you have in your garage? Is it going to matter how big your house is or how high your stacks of money are? What good will any of it do you then?

It won't be worth anything.

The fact is nobody gets to the end of life and says, "Man, I just wish I would have spent less time with my family so I could have worked more hours to earn more money to buy more stuff."

Nobody says, "My one regret in life is that I only had *two* vacation homes."

People don't care about those things at the end of their lives. And you won't care about them either.

Instead, what you'll want is to have good things to look back on. Memories, experiences, stories of a life well-lived.

You will want to remember the friends and family you had, the people you loved and who loved you. You'll want to reminisce about your adventures, your trials, the times you went up against impossible odds and came out on top. You'll want to relive the most meaningful moments of your life. You'll want to laugh and cry and then laugh some more.

You'll want good stories, ones that weren't copied from television or popular culture but were written with your sweat and tears and laughter, custom built to your specifications.

My question is, if we are going to want those things at the end of our lives, why don't we purposely live our lives in such a way as to get those things?

Why do we spend so much of our time focusing on success, which won't matter to us, and so little of our time on our stories?

In his book *The 7 Habits of Highly Effective People*, Stephen Covey says that successful people "begin with the end in mind." In other words, they live their lives backwards. They think through their end goals and aspirations, then they line the rest of their actions up with those goals. That's what true success is: not money and fame and power, but a life well-lived.

If you want a life full of good stories, you have to begin with the end in mind. You have to decide what sort of stories you want to tell, and then you have to live your life in such a way as to create those stories.

That's what I try to do. If I am in a situation where I have an opportunity to live a good story, a story I will want to tell later on, I make sure to do it, even if it is embarrassing or difficult at the time. I don't want to regret the missed opportunity.

For instance, several years ago I spent about six months of my life calling the White House almost every day.

I had been at a thrift store, and there was this book called *Hundreds of Things to Do on a Rainy Day*. It was exactly that, just a list of all these things you could do. But one of the items on the list said, "Call the White House." And it listed a phone number below it.

At first I thought, "How cool would that be?" But when I considered how old the book was, I decided the information was probably outdated.

Then on second thought, I realized the White House had not *moved* during that time. There wasn't really a reason for them to have a different number. So I called it.

"White House." said the lady on the other end, who had answered much sooner than I had expected. I hesitated.

"White House?" I said back.

"White House." she said.

"Like... *the* White House?" I said back.

She said, "Yes, sir. This is *the* White House. How may I help you?"

That was when I realized I did not really have a reason for calling the White House. I hadn't really thought the plan through in advance. So I just said what anyone else would've said in the same circumstance.

"Um...I need to speak with the President, please."

Before I even got the sentence out of my mouth, the lady said, "Sir, the President is unavailable to take your call at this time." You could tell she'd had this conversation before.

I thought for a moment, then said, "Well, could you page me through to his cell phone or something? It's really important."

"Sir, the President *is unavailable to take your call at this time*." she said again, a little meaner this time.

And then she hung up on me. The President's secretary hung up on me.

And that was when I realized that this was not the White House number. I mean technically this lady was probably sitting in the White House answering the phone, and it probably even said "White House" on her paycheck and everything, but this was not the *real* number. There was no phone line connecting this number to the big red phone on the President's desk. This was the number they gave out so idiots like me could prank call the White House.

So that's what I did. Almost every day, for about six months. Whenever I was driving home from school or work, when most people turn on the radio and zone out, I would use that time to prank call the White House.

When say I prank called the White House, I don't mean that I called them and asked if their refrigerator was running. I just called with really stupid questions. All the time.

I called once during the Olympics, when the United States basketball team was losing to countries I had never even heard of.

"White House." the lady answered, as usual.

"Um, yeah... I was just calling to see what in the world is going on with our basketball players?"

This caught her off guard. She paused for a second,

thinking perhaps I had dialed the wrong number.

"Excuse me?" she said.

"The US basketball team. We are losing to countries that I am pretty sure are not even real countries. It looks like they just got a bunch of guys from a YMCA pickup team and made up a country name that sounded convincing." I said.

"Huh?" she asked, still confused.

"The Olympics!" I said. "We *invented* basketball! Why is this happening?"

"Sir, this is the White House..." she said.

"I know. You said that at the beginning." I said.

"But..." she trailed off for a second. "...why are you calling the White House about this?" she asked.

"Because it's the *United States basketball team.*" I said. "Who else am I going to call?"

"Sir," she said, obviously a little annoyed. "We have nothing to do with any of that."

I paused for a second.

"I bet you wouldn't be saying that if we were winning." I said.

Then she hung up on me, as usual.

I was used to it though because this happened every time. I was kind of hoping if I called enough times, just *maybe* the President would call me back. Maybe all the members of the White House staff would be standing around at the water cooler talking about their day, and the President would overhear someone talking about this crazy guy who keeps calling every day with stupid questions.

And then maybe the President would say, "Who is this guy? What's his name?"

And the lady would say, "Kyle Scheele." (I assumed the White House had caller ID).

And then maybe the President would be in the mood for having some fun and he would say, "I've got a couple minutes before I have to get back to my duties. Let's call this guy just to mess with him."

But it didn't happen. And eventually I got concerned that perhaps my name was going to be put on some sort of list that would come back and haunt me later in life. I pictured the Secret Service kicking down my door in the middle of the night, dragging me kicking and screaming to some faraway prison for people who think it is funny to waste the President's time.

I pictured living out the rest of my life in a lonely cell away from my friends and family, like that guy in *The Count of Monte Cristo*, marking my days with tiny scratches on the walls of my cell. The only thing in the cell would be a phone, but it couldn't make outbound calls, and several times a day the lady from the White House would prank call me just to laugh at my misfortune, her laugh deep and echoing, a haunting sort of "*muahahaha...*"

So I stopped calling.

But those stories did exactly what I wanted them to. They made people laugh. I've probably told those stories a thousand times. People I don't even know will come up to me and say, "You're Kyle, right? One of your friends was telling me about the time you prank called the White House!" Then they will want me to tell it all over again.

I could have just thought about doing it. I could have lied and said that I did. But I wanted the stories to be real. And if you want stories to be real, you actually have to live them. If you want a meaningful life, you actually have to do meaningful things.

That's kind of a silly example, but the analogy is solid. We have to live the stories we want to tell. We have to get off the couch and do these things.

We have to prank call the President.

# 7

## The Kind of Stories You Want to Read

ONCE YOU START THINKING ABOUT LIFE THIS way, things get interesting fast. You start running up against people who think you are crazy, who want you to accept the status quo, people who have a certain vision of what they think your life should look like and who are offended when you choose to live it differently.

Part of choosing to live a better story is learning to care less about what other people think. When you realize you only get one shot at this, you begin to focus on making it count instead of making it please someone else.

But the thing is, the less you care about what other people think, the more those people get upset that you don't care. People begin to say things about you that are ridiculous simply because they don't understand what you are doing.

For instance, whenever you decide to ignore everyone else and live the best story you can, some people will call you selfish. They will say you are putting your own wants and needs ahead of everyone else's, that you should come down from your high horse.

And that almost sounds true until you think about what they are actually saying, what their words are implying.

Because if doing what you love is selfish, then selflessness would mean doing what you hate, doing stuff you don't care about, stuff you have no desire to do. And that's ridiculous.

What virtue is there in doing things that you hate? I never understand people who complain about their job but never make any effort to get a different one. It's strange because I know that somewhere out there is a different person who would love to have that job, but they can't because it's being taken up by someone who hates it.

When you think about it, staying at a job you hate is actually *more* selfish than doing what you love, because it keeps someone else from their dream. If everyone is doing things they hate, why don't we all just switch and do the things we love? Wouldn't that make more sense?

Of course, this analogy breaks down at a certain point. We can't all do what we love all the time. No matter who you are or what your job is, there will be parts of your life that are dull and unexciting but still necessary. Paying your taxes isn't glamorous, but you have to do it. Most people do not find joy in brushing their teeth, but we should all brush our teeth nonetheless. Paying bills and taking care of our responsibilities are things we all have to do, *especially* if we're going to live a good story. You can't get around this.

And yes, there *are* selfish ways of pursuing your dreams. Mooching off your parents or the government while you try to launch your rock and roll career is selfish. Don't do

76

that. Get a job, pay your bills, and pursue your rockstar gig with your own time and money.

If your dream comes at the cost of someone else's time or money or hard work, you're a jerk. And you're not living a good story.

But if you're covering your responsibilities and not placing a burden on the people around you, then you should feel free to pursue the story you want. People may not agree with you, but that's their problem.

I am not saying you should ignore everyone, either. That's a surefire recipe for disaster. What I am saying is that you should listen to the voices of people who care about you, people who want the best for you, who are encouraging you and pushing you towards the things that you love. If those people have criticism for you, you should listen to it because those are the voices worth listening to. But if the criticism is coming from someone who is generally negative, someone who doesn't even seem to enjoy his *own* life, then certainly don't let his opinion influence yours.

The truth is this: nothing great ever comes from people who hate what they are doing. No one begrudgingly paints a masterpiece. People do not write bestselling novels because someone tells them they have to.

Instead, the best things in the world come from people who create the sorts of things they are passionate about, who build the things they think are missing from the world.

Sixty or seventy years ago, two fellows in Britain started building a friendship around a shared love of Norse mythology. They talked about their favorite books, about what made them so good, about how there weren't enough stories like that anymore.

But instead of just lamenting the loss of good stories, they decided to write some stories like the ones they loved. They weren't trying to get rich, weren't even trying to get published. Neither one of them even thought their stories were very good, that anybody else would really care about them. But they liked them enough to keep working on them, to keep writing, to keep crafting the kinds of stories that had captivated them as children.

Those two men were C.S. Lewis and J.R.R. Tolkien. The stories they wrote were *The Chronicles of Narnia* and *The Lord of the Rings,* stories that have captivated generations of readers, spawned numerous hit movies, and together sold over 250 million copies.

That story reminds me of one of my favorite quotes, one from a guy named Howard Thurman, who said, "Don't ask what the world needs. Ask what makes you come alive, and go do it. Because what the world needs is people who have come alive."

C.S. Lewis and J.R.R. Tolkien did just that. They didn't write stories because they thought there was a good market for them (although it turned out there was). They didn't write fantasy stories because fantasy stories were particularly popular at the time (they weren't). They just wrote the kinds of stories they loved, the kinds of stories that made them come alive. And it turns out the world needed those kinds of stories after all.

Contrast this with what happened after *Harry Potter* got big. People started saying "Hey, books about kid wizards are popular right now. I should write a book about a kid wizard!" And suddenly the market was flooded with books about kid wizards.

Same thing with *Twilight.* Did you notice how many vampire and werewolf romance novels came out after *Twilight?* They were everywhere.

Do you remember these books? Not in general, but specifically. Do you remember any of their titles? Do you remember any of their characters or plot lines? Do you remember staying up until midnight to buy the next book in the series the minute it was released?

I doubt it. You know why? Because they weren't written by people who loved kid wizards or vampire love stories.

It is one thing to be inspired by someone else. There is nothing wrong with that. The book you are holding would not exist if it weren't for other books that inspired me, books by people like Donald Miller and Joseph Campbell and C.S. Lewis and others. But this book is also unique, and it's full of my own stories, my own lessons, my own experiences.

I don't know if this book will sell ten copies, ten thousand, or ten million. But I know that regardless of any of that, I will be proud that I wrote it because I know it's mine. I know it's the book I wanted to write.

When I think about people who write ripoff stories it makes me sad because writing a book is really hard. It takes a lot of time and effort and energy. And that goes for any book, whether it's the one you wanted to write or the one you thought would sell a lot of copies.

That's the thing. You are going to spend the time either way. Those seconds and minutes and days and weeks are not sticking around. And in the time it takes to write the story where the vampire falls in love with the kid wizard, you could have written the story you wanted to write, the one that makes you happy.

The same is true of our lives. The next five years are going to pass at the same rate whether you spend them pursuing your dreams or pursuing someone else's. Either way, they'll be gone forever. You will never have a chance to do them over.

When I was in high school, I played basketball, football, and tennis. A three-sport athlete! The only problem was, I was terrible at sports (Actually, I'm still terrible at sports.).

The only reason I made any of the teams was because I was funny and I kept the other players pumped up, so the coaches gave me a jersey and let me keep the bench warm. But whenever I actually got put in the game, things went bad in a hurry.

Once, our basketball team was playing a game against a team that was made up entirely of guys who were just as hopeless as I was. In fact, they were so bad that we would only use four of our players on defense, and we would keep one guy back on our side of the court. Once we stole the ball or got the rebound, we would throw our guy a pass and he would make an easy basket.

On one trip down the court, it was my turn to be the guy who stayed back and made the basket. I hung back at our three point line, waiting for one of my teammates to pass me the ball. Like clockwork, the other team missed their shot, our team got the rebound, and our point guard threw the ball down the court to me.

To this day I am not exactly sure what happened next. All I know is that as I tried to turn around, run, and catch the ball at the same time, I managed to do none of those things.

Instead, my feet got tangled together, my arms reached out for the ball, and I fell flat on my face in front of everyone. The ball went out of bounds, the other team got possession back, and my teammates stood there shaking their heads.

I fell so hard, the referee actually had to stop the game TWICE to make sure I was okay. Finally my coach pulled me out of the game and asked, "What happened out there?" and I jokingly said, "I think I must have tripped over one of the lines on the court."

For the rest of my high school career, any time I was in or near a gymnasium, people would say, "Hey Scheele, watch out for those lines!" I graduated high school eight years ago, and to this day when I run into old friends they will say, "Tripped over any lines lately?"

Finally, my senior year, I quit playing sports altogether. I realized I wasn't any good at it, and more importantly, I realized it wasn't really that important to me. I didn't have any desire to be an athlete. What I loved was getting people excited about things. So I got together with a bunch of my other non-sport-playing friends and we started dressing up in crazy costumes for all of the football games.

The first time we dressed up was for a game against a team called the Branson Pirates. We figured since they were Pirates we would dress up as the Coast Guard. So we did. And the crowd went nuts. We even got interviewed for the local paper.

After that, we started dressing up for every game. And when football season ended, we dressed up for basketball games. Sometimes our costumes had to do with the other team, sometimes not. Once we got kicked out of a Taco Bell because the guy said our togas violated the "No shirts,

No shoes, No service" policy.

Word got out about our little unofficial pep squad, and other schools took notice. Somebody on one of the other teams was quoted saying, "Those pretty boys out in the crowd aren't going to know what hit them."

We thought that was hilarious so we started calling ourselves the Pretty Boyz (we added the z for a little extra pizzazz). By the end of the year we had been in the newspaper more times than our football and basketball teams combined. We even got our own picture in the school yearbook with all of the official clubs and organizations. It was ridiculous.

Obviously there is nothing wrong with playing sports. Both of my brothers were good enough athletes to play in college, but I guess I missed out on that gene. I have had lots of friends who were very good at sports and really loved it. But for me, playing sports was something I did because I thought I was supposed to, because it seemed like a story that had worked for other people. But it never worked for me.

If I had stayed with that story, I never would have gotten to be a part of the Pretty Boyz. I never would have gotten my picture in the paper, never would have gotten kicked out of a Taco Bell, never would have made the great memories that I did. More importantly, I never would have followed the path of doing crazy things that get other people excited, which has turned into a career for me now. Instead, I would have spent the whole time sitting on the bench, trying to live a story that wasn't mine.

# 8

## —— Just Like the Movies ——

WHENEVER I SPEAK TO TEENAGERS ABOUT THIS kind of stuff, there is always someone in the audience who is thinking, "That sounds nice Kyle, but you don't know my situation."

I can tell they are thinking this because they are sitting with their arms crossed tightly, head tilted to one side, brows raised high over squinting eyes. And that sort of body language can only mean one thing.

It means they are thinking, "It won't work for me. I have too many obstacles keeping me from a good story. You don't know my situation." Either that or they are having digestive problems and they don't want to be rude by leaving during the middle of my talk.

You might be thinking the same thing at this point (about the obstacles, not the digestion). And you would be right, at least partially.

I don't know your situation. Depending on who you are, I may not know anything about you. We may have never met. Or perhaps we have met, but only briefly. Perhaps I would not recognize you on the street or remember your name. Or perhaps I would recognize you but not remember your name, in which case I would say, "Hey buddy!" or "Hello, old friend!"

But that's beside the point. The point is that your situation is not relevant.

See, most of us think we're the exception to the rule. Most of us like to think we are the one unique case where living a better story isn't a possibility.

But the truth is, you're probably not. There may be one guy in the world who has the odds so stacked against him that it is actually not possible for him to live a better story, but I've never met him. And even if he exists, which I doubt, I can guarantee you're not him.

How do I know? Because I have heard too many stories. I have heard too many stories of people who have had it far worse than you could ever imagine, people whose lives were so terrible you and I probably couldn't comprehend it, but who managed to make something of themselves nonetheless.

I've heard stories of people who were blind, deaf, mute, or any combination of the three.

Stories of people born without arms and legs.

Stories of people born with arms and legs they subsequently parted with.

People imprisoned under false pretenses.

People imprisoned for perfectly good reasons.

People who were paralyzed, or partially paralyzed, or temporarily paralyzed.

People who suffered abuse, or neglect, or poverty, or who were mentally or physically or emotionally handicapped.

And in all of these stories, though there were moments of great pain and struggle, there were also moments of great meaning, moments where setbacks and limitations were overcome. And for many of these people, the pain in their lives ended up being the very thing that gave them an opportunity to live an amazing story.

The truth is, there is nothing you are going through that hasn't happened to someone else at some point. And yes, some of those people were so wrecked by it that they were never the same again. But some of the others were able to dust themselves off and carry on living. And they didn't just get back to their old lives, either. Instead, they used the experience to push themselves to be better people.

In the end, which of these groups you fall into is entirely up to you.

I'm not saying it's going to be easy. I'm just saying it's possible. And deep down, you know I am right. You know that the setbacks in your life can be overcome. You know that none of this has to be permanent. But you also know it is going to be difficult, that it would be a lot easier to play it safe and be the victim, to tell yourself you are the exception, that this won't work for you. But that's not true.

If nothing else, our culture tells us it's not true. Look around you. What are the movies that affect us most as a culture? They're the Cinderella stories, the come-from-behind last-second wins, the victories against unfathomable odds. Those are the stories that resonate with something deep inside of us because they show us there is still hope despite our circumstances.

Those stories can be a great inspiration for us. They can show us what is possible and inspire us to reach for it. But they can be more than that, too. They can be instructive. They can show us *how* to live better stories.

See, there's a formula to these movies, an underlying structure that exists in every single one. And I don't even have to tell it to you. You already know it. I'll prove it to you.

Say you're watching a movie about a boxer. In the first five minutes of the movie, the guy is getting the crap kicked out of him. Every fight he's in, he loses. Bad. His home life is falling apart, he can't pay his bills, everything is going south for this guy.

If that happens in the first five minutes of the movie, what is going to happen in the last five minutes?

I don't even have to say it. You already know. The guy wins the HEAVYWEIGHT CHAMPIONSHIP OF THE WORLD!

Or say it's a football movie. The movie opens on this high school team from the middle of nowhere (It's always somewhere in Texas. Don't ask me why, I don't make the rules.) They have a new coach and the team isn't doing well at all. They are bickering and dropping passes and running the wrong plays. Three of the guys are fighting over the same cheerleader girlfriend and another guy is about to fail his classes and lose his eligibility. Their first game is a total embarrassment as the other team runs all over them on their home field.

Again, if that is what happens in the first five minutes, what happens in the last five minutes? You know it, right? This little high school team goes on to win the Super Bowl, despite not even being in the league or meeting the minimum age requirements!

It's strange, because we all know what is going to happen in those movies. When you hear there is a new football movie coming out, do you have any doubt who will win the game at the end? When you hear about a new boxing movie, you know the guy is going to win the title fight, right? But it doesn't stop the story from being fascinating, from keeping you on the edge of your seat.

Predictability isn't a bad thing. Boring stories are a bad thing.

Most of the best stories are pretty predictable, actually. There's a formula to them: take whatever pain or struggle is present in the beginning of the movie, turn it on its head, make it positive, and that's what happens at the end. That's where the story ends up. It works for football movies and boxing movies and romance movies and all sorts of others.

And that formula works for you and me, too. It helps us to make sense of the pain elements in our stories, helps us to turn them into something meaningful.

So many times when pain enters our lives, we let that pain be the end of our story. Even if we don't say it out loud or think of it that way, it's how we feel. We stop reaching out, stop aiming for bigger things, stop trying for a better life. We think, "I tried living a better story and this is what happened." So we decide to play it safe and coast through life instead.

But those kinds of stories always turn out to be pretty crappy. No offense, but they do. If you went to a movie and it was about a kid who got bullied, and then for the rest of the movie nothing else happened and the kid never overcame that, wouldn't you think the movie was pretty dumb? Or if you saw a movie about a kid who was mistreated by his parents, but then for the rest of the movie he just went around holding a grudge about it and never moved past that to do bigger things, wouldn't you want your money back once the credits rolled?

It's not that you don't have a right to hold a grudge, to refuse to let go of the pain someone caused you. It's your life. You have every right to do that. It just won't make for a very good story because you're letting the wrong people win. If you don't overcome the pain in your life, the people who caused you that pain get the last laugh. And stories where the bad guy prevails do not tend to win Oscars.

Yes, bad things have happened to you that are not your fault. Yes, those things brought pain and consequences that you did not ask for. Yes, they were caused by other people. But if you wait around for those people to come back and fix what they have broken, you are going to be waiting an awfully long time.

When you start to think of life as a story, like a movie or a book or something told around a campfire, it causes you to live differently. You don't let sources of pain be the end of your story, for one thing. Instead, you let the pain be the impetus for living a better story, let it move you to action. You let the pain be the beginning of a newer and far richer story. Oddly enough, the pain often becomes something you are thankful for because it was the first step in a journey that takes you far beyond the story you used to live.

The easy way to do this, to figure out the direction your life should take, is to look at the pain elements in your story. What is the biggest source of hurt in your life? Is it your parents? Your friends (or lack thereof)? Your handicap? Is it a specific thing that happened to you? Is it something you did that you can't forgive yourself for? What is it for you?

Then once you have pinpointed the things that have hurt you, imagine you were to see those things happen to someone in the first five minutes of a movie. How would you expect that person to change by the end of the movie? Where would you expect them to end up?

Then move towards that.

This is a good exercise because it removes us from the equation. It is no longer a story about *me*, it's a story about a character in a movie. And when it's just about some character, I am free to imagine all sorts of possibilities I might never consider in my own life, free to think of solutions that might not be obvious in my own circumstances because I am too close to the situation.

I am convinced that most of us know the right thing to do most of the time. We are not idiots. The problem is that we often aren't able to look at things objectively, to remove our own motives and excuses from the equation. When the situation is about us, we find all sorts of ways to rationalize our bad behavior, to make excuses for our poor efforts, to reason our way out of our obligation to make something beautiful from our pain.

This is why we are often able to give others the advice we can't take ourselves. It's why it is easy for you to tell your friend she should break up with her jerk boyfriend but hard to see that you should probably do the same. It's why it is easy for you to give someone else advice on their diet while you are eating an entire cake.

But when you view yourself as a character in a story,

you suddenly become acutely aware of exactly what you should do.

Imagining yourself as a character in a story seems like the sort of thing a crazy person would do. It seems like living in a fantasy world or something, like the sort of thing that wouldn't be healthy. And maybe that's true. All I know is that it works.

In a way, I suppose this is the opposite of what Ryan was doing by stealing stories from Polaroid commercials. Ryan was trying to pull false stories into reality, and in doing so he contaminated what was real. What I am suggesting is the reverse. Instead of pretending that a commercial or a movie is your life (and thereby living a lie), you pretend your life is a movie, that you are a character in that movie, and that you have a story to tell.

Then you tell yourself that story until you grow into it, until it molds to fit you like a baseball mitt that's been broken in.

# 9

## —— Walking Down Hallways ——

A FEW PAGES BACK I SAID THAT VIEWING YOUR life as a story will help you know what to do next. And that's true. But perhaps more importantly, it will also help you to know what NOT to do next.

See, great stories are great not just for what is put into them, but also for what is left out.

Remember that great scene in *Lord of the Rings* where Sam and Frodo are on their epic quest to destroy the ring and defeat Sauron, but they take a break from all of that to go to that water park in Mordor?

I'll never forget seeing Gollum tubing down the lazy river, sipping frozen lemonade out of one of those cups with a little umbrella, or watching Samwise go down that twisty water slide and shoot out into the pool full of Orc children at the bottom, grinning from ear to ear like a little kid. Man, what a great scene!

Remember that? Oh. Me neither.

See, a scene like that would never even make it into the

first draft of a script. It doesn't belong in a story like *Lord of the Rings*. It wouldn't make any sense. And even though it could be really funny, and maybe there could even be some memorable moments in there if it was written by somebody with talent, it would ultimately still be a huge distraction from the rest of the film.

Most of the time these things don't make it into movies and books because they get edited out. But every now and then one slips through the editing process and you'll see a scene in a movie or read a few pages of a book and think, "Huh? What was that all about?"

We recognize these things in other people's stories, in movies and books and on television. We recognize when characters are doing the wrong things, when the story seems to be losing its direction. But we don't always recognize these things in our own lives. We don't always see when our own stories are getting off track.

Have you ever noticed that nobody pees on television?

I don't mean peeing *onto* a television, because that would be dangerous and would ruin a perfectly good TV. What I mean is that you never see somebody on TV stop in the middle of a conversation and say, "Hold that thought. Sorry to interrupt, but I've gotta pee!"

That happens all the time in real life, especially if you have a small bladder like me. But it never happens on TV.

You never see people on TV eat, either. I mean, sometimes you'll see a family having a meal together, or two people at a restaurant on a date, but they're really just talking. You never see a guy alone in a kitchen, getting out some bread and peanut butter and jelly, and then he makes a sandwich, and then for five minutes you just watch him eat the sandwich.

Last but not least, people never sleep on TV. A few years ago there was this show called 24, one of those action-adventure sorts of shows where somebody was always kidnapping the President or trying to blow up the White House or something. Each episode was one hour in the story, and there were 24 episodes in a season, so the whole season was basically just one day from start to finish.

But the weird thing was, nobody ever slept on that show. That seemed strange to me since the average person needs about eight hours of sleep every night. By that rule, every season should've had eight episodes in a row where the main guy was just asleep.

But they never had *any* episodes like that. These people never slept at all. They never ate or peed either. How do you go an entire day without peeing?!

The answer, of course, is you don't. I don't even know if it's possible. But it's television, so it doesn't have to be possible. It just has to be entertaining.

That's the reason they don't show any of this stuff on television. Because it's not entertaining. It's boring. It doesn't advance the story at all. And if it doesn't advance the story, it gets cut.

See, the screenwriters know they only have a certain amount of time to tell their stories. If the TV show is 30 minutes long and 11 minutes of that is for commercials, they know they've got 19 minutes to tell the story. But the problem is that a good story won't fit into 19 minutes. If you include everything that actually happens in real life, all of the peeing and eating and sleeping, the story would be way too long.

So the screenwriters have to trim out anything that isn't directly advancing the story they are trying to tell. They can only include the things that push the story forward.

In one sense, the screenwriters have an advantage over us: they know how much time they have. They know exactly how long each story will end up being.

You and I have limited timelines for our stories too. It's true. New statistics are coming back that say one out of every one person is going to die. It's pretty depressing, to be honest.

The bummer for us is that none of us know when it is going to happen. None of us know how long we have left. None of us have any idea when the credits are going to roll on our stories.

When I was in high school, I had a friend named Nathan (Not the one who stole my popcorn in chapter six. Different Nathan.). Nathan and I were not close friends or anything, but we played on the tennis team together, were in some of the same clubs, and had some of the same classes. He was always a really funny guy, a little mischievous but always really kind to everyone.

One day Nathan was walking down the hallway at school, carrying some boxes of chocolate for a fundraiser. Just walking down the hallway. Not the sort of situation that you would ever remember except that as he was walking, a blood vessel burst inside of his brain and he fell to the ground.

Within half an hour, he had gone blind.

Before he was taken from the school in a helicopter, he was on oxygen.

By the time he arrived at the hospital, he was brain dead.

And by the time school started the next day, the doctors had donated his organs and taken him off of life support.

Walking down the hallway, and his story was over. Done.

Luckily, Nathan had lived a pretty great story. He was a really happy kid, had a great relationship with his family, was really involved in his school and his church. At his funeral, all of his friends and classmates were there, and there were a lot of tears. But there was also a lot of laughter, a lot of smiles as stories were told and pictures were shown. His life had been short, but very, very full.

Contrast that with another student who died in my high school. I won't print his name here out of respect for his family, but he was a student in my class. One night he was partying with some friends, drinking and doing drugs at someone's house. At some point in the night he passed out and began to turn blue. His friends didn't want to stop partying though so they pushed him under a table, thinking that maybe he just needed to sleep it off. He never woke up again. Dead from alcohol poisoning at the age of 17.

I hadn't known him as well as I had known Nathan, hadn't had classes together or interacted very much. But I remember when he died, I listened to the stories people told, the things they remembered about him. And they were all from when he was much younger, memories from grade school and the early years of adolescence, memories about riding bikes together and playing on the playground.

But as he got older, it seemed, his life became less and

less memorable. He began to hang out with the sorts of people who are content to live stories that are forgettable. When he died, no one told any stories about the last part of his life, the part that should have been freshest in their memories. I remember being puzzled about this, about feeling a sort of sadness about the whole thing. And I didn't even know the guy.

I'm sure he thought he would get his life together later, that he'd spend a few years going through his hard-partying phase, doing drugs and heavy drinking and all of that, and then eventually he would settle down and get a job and raise a family, telling his kids not to do the sorts of things he had done. But he never got the chance to do any of that.

And that's the thing about life. None of us know how much time is on the clock. None of us really have any idea of when we're going to die.

In sports, people play hardest right at the end, when the clock is winding down and the buzzer is about to sound. They give extra effort then because they know they won't have another chance later. And I think if we knew how much time we had left, we would probably play harder too. We'd probably live much more intentionally knowing that time was running out and there wouldn't be a chance to do it over.

I think if that kid had known he would die so young, he probably would have made a point to live a better story. And the sad thing is that by living a better story he would have probably chosen not to do the things that ended up killing him. Because when the clock is running out, getting drunk is probably not at the top of your bucket list.

The morning he died, I don't think he woke up thinking, "Today's the day! Better make it count!" And when Nathan left his classroom to carry those boxes of chocolate, I don't think he knew he would never make it to the end of the hallway. I don't think he had any idea. But that didn't stop what happened. It didn't change the fact that his time was up, his story finished.

I wonder how you and I would live differently if we were really conscious of the fact that our lives could end at any moment, that we are each one burst blood vessel away from the end. I wonder how we would treat people, how we would spend our time and our money and our energy. I wonder the sorts of things we would do or not do, the things we would say or left unsaid.

I think if we are honest, we would live a lot differently. I think we would live with more intention, more purpose, more meaning.

I think we would live a lot better stories.

# 10

## —— Here Lies John Smith ——

I MENTIONED EARLIER THAT I'VE NEVER MET anyone at the end of his life who said, "I wish I had more cars and houses and money."

And that's true. But I've also never met anyone who said, "Looking back, I wish I had checked my email more. I wish I had updated my Facebook status just *one* more time." I don't think people say, "If I had to do it all over, I would go back and get three stars on every level of Angry Birds. That's my one regret."

When people are lying on their deathbeds, surrounded by friends and family, reminiscing the best days of their lives, I doubt they stop and say, "Sorry. This is so emotional... I've gotta tweet this."

It's funny when you think about it that way, when you imagine someone actually saying these things. But it's not funny when you realize this is how we spend so much of our lives. It's not funny when you think about all of the ways we waste our time, all of the things we are going to look back on and regret. It's not funny at all. It's just sad.

When I think about some of the things I have wasted time on, the time spent surfing the internet and playing video games, the checking and rechecking of Facebook and Twitter and all the rest, it makes me a little sick to my stomach because I know that none of this stuff will matter in fifty years, that most of it won't matter in fifty days. Truth be told, most of it doesn't even matter now.

So why do we do this stuff?

Simple: Because it is easier to do these things than to do things that matter, easier to live these stories than to live better ones. There is an addicting simplicity to this stuff, a sort of numbing of the senses that comes as we retread the same steps we have taken a thousand times before.

When I think about my concerns for future generations, for my kids and their kids and the ones who come after, these are the things I am worried about. Not that they will ruin their lives, but that they will waste them.

Whenever I meet someone and they find out I'm a youth speaker, they inevitably say something like, "Oh, so you tell kids not to drink and do drugs?"

And I suppose if a student said, "Hey man, I've been thinking about getting into drugs. What are your thoughts?" I would tell him not to. But that is not my main concern. That is not the thing I am most worried about. Students hear plenty about that stuff all the time.

If anything, I worry about how *much* we tell students not to drink and do drugs, not to drive fast or have sex or gossip or steal. I'm worried we spend so much time talking about these things that we are teaching our young people to define their lives by all of the things they *don't* do.

See, it is possible to live a life where you don't drink or do drugs, don't text while driving or smoke cigarettes, where you don't cheat on tests or cheat on boyfriends or break the speed limit or the law... It is possible to live a life where you don't do any of those things, but you don't do much of anything else either.

It's not that I want you to do any of that stuff, because I don't. I don't think those things will make your life any better. But I am far more concerned with what you put into your story than what you leave out. I would much rather hear about all of the things you have done than the things you haven't.

I'm worried we spend so much time warning our young people about the things that could *take* their lives, and no time warning them about the things that can *waste* them. I'm worried we are raising up a generation whose tombstones will read, "Here lies John Smith, who never did much of anything."

It seems like adults these days spend a lot of time complaining about young people, about their lack of direction, how they don't seem to be as driven as young people in the past. To be honest, I don't know if that is true or not, because I am still pretty young myself so I don't have very much to compare with. Most of the students I interact with are pretty cool though.

But even if it is true, I wonder how much of that is our own fault. I wonder how much of it has to do with the fact that we spend more time telling students how *not* to live their lives than we do showing them what a well-lived life looks like.

When I was younger, I loved cheap, greasy food. I used to eat it all the time. But I didn't just eat it because it was cheap and convenient... I genuinely liked the stuff. And I remember when parents and teachers would talk about how bad the stuff is for you, how it is full of empty calories and probably made from ground-up cats and all of that. But I didn't really care, because I thought it was delicious. And I have never been a fan of cats anyways, so I figured they probably had it coming.

At some point though, I stopped eating fast food. I hardly do it at all anymore, and when I do, I don't really enjoy it. And it's not because I finally came to my senses about how unhealthy it was. It's not because enough people told me not to eat it that I finally gave in.

You know what it was? My wife started making really healthy food at home. Things that came from the ground, animals that were very recently alive. Fresh fruits and vegetables, chicken that was not soaked in butter for a month, that sort of thing. And I found I really liked all of it. And after that, fast food didn't seem as good anymore.

To tell the truth, it didn't happen overnight. I didn't even realize it was happening. When I first started eating healthy food, I thought I could keep loving both.

But then one day my wife was hanging out with some friends and I was on my own for dinner. I picked up something cheap and fast, the sort of thing I used to love. I was surprised to find I didn't like it very much. At first I thought that perhaps I had gotten a bad burger, that this particular fry chef had not been at the top of his game that day. But the next time I ate fast food it was the same thing. And the next time after that. And eventually I realized I just don't like the stuff anymore.

I don't think the food changed at all. I am sure the recipes are all the same as they always were: one part cat, one part salt, one part lard, then stir over low heat until all the hair burns off. The recipes are the same, but I am not. Once I got a taste for better stuff, the old stuff didn't satisfy me anymore.

That experience makes me wonder if maybe we have been approaching this entire thing the wrong way. I wonder if we have spent too much time telling students what *not* to do when we should have just shown them how to live better stories. Because when they start to live better stories, they won't have a taste for any of that stuff anymore.

My friend Ellie is like that. She is a really cool girl, very accomplished for how young she is. She just graduated high school last year, but already she has taken three trips to help refugees in other countries, and she volunteers a lot of her time to raise money for them. She helped plan a big event last year that raised enough money to build a bunch of houses in a refugee camp in El Salvador. She does this in addition to her normal life, where she goes to school and has a job and volunteers at her church and hangs out with friends. And on top of all that, she is a very talented singer who spends a lot of time practicing guitar and voice.

The stuff that Ellie is doing is so impacting, so meaningful, I don't think she has given drugs and alcohol a second thought. I just don't think that stuff would appeal to her on any level because it would be a huge step down from the life she has now.

I have known Ellie's family for a long time now. Back before I was married, when my wife-to-be moved to town, Ellie's family let her live with them so she wouldn't have to pay rent on an apartment somewhere. So while Lindsay and I were dating, we spent a lot of time with Ellie's family, eating meals together and watching movies and observing how they all interacted.

And you know what I never saw? I never saw Ellie's parents talk to her about drugs or alcohol or sex one time. I never heard them warn her about "destructive decisions" or any of that. I'm sure it has happened once or twice because they are parents and they have to cover those bases just to be safe, but it's not something they seemed to spend a lot of time on.

Instead, I saw them encouraging Ellie to get involved in the things she loved. When she wanted to learn to play guitar, they helped her find a guitar and get lessons and schedule practice time. When she wanted to sing, they got her involved in the choir at church. When she wanted to help refugees in other countries, they encouraged her in that. And it seems like that strategy has worked out pretty well so far.

I am not a fortune-teller (mainly because the uniform is ridiculous), so I can't tell the future. Even so, I would bet money that Ellie ends up with a great story at the end of her life. And it won't be because somebody told her not to do a bunch of stuff.

This principle explains what happens when someone goes on a crazy diet. If the diet says not to eat carbs, people will find a way to eat the most unhealthy carb-free foods they can find. They'll be downing slabs of bacon and pork-chop smoothies and eating butter without bread. They may lose weight since they are causing crazy nutritional imbalances in their bodies, but they aren't any healthier.

I think that's the danger in focusing on what *not* to do. There is a strong possibility that you will keep taking things out and never put anything better in. And in the end you will have just traded one bad story for another.

Instead of taking out all of the things we think are unhealthy, maybe we should just spend more time putting healthier things in. When you keep putting more and more meaning into your life, more and more experiences that actually matter, all of the other stuff will get pushed to the margins. It will become less appealing. And when your life finally gets so full that something has to go, there won't be any question of what is first on the chopping block.

I have never been a guy who struggled with drugs or alcohol or any of the things that we are warned to stay away from. But there are other things that I fight against, lesser addictions that are still dangerous, things that waste my life and steal my time.

And when I look back on my life, on the times when I have been most free from the death grip of video games and the internet and social media triviality, it hasn't been when I knuckled down and tried my hardest to give up those things. It has been when I've been too busy doing better things.

A few years ago I went down to New Orleans to help in the aftermath of Hurricane Katrina. I was there for a week helping victims clean up their houses and get their lives back together and that sort of thing. It was backbreaking work from sunup to sundown, day after day after day, the kind of thing where you would fall asleep from sheer exhaustion before your head even hit the pillow. But I loved every second of it.

And you know what? The whole time I was there, I didn't check my email one time, didn't update my Facebook status or watch any internet videos of cats playing the piano.

And to be honest with you, I didn't miss it one bit.

# 11

## —— Timeless Classics ——

SOME STORIES ARE REALLY GOOD, BUT ONLY for about ten minutes. For whatever reason, they have a very brief shelf life before they lose their appeal.

Pop culture is built around stories like these. Everything has to be very current, very what's-happening-right-now, or else it gets thrown out. The turnover rate is ridiculous. If you were to go back and watch old late night shows from five or ten years ago, you probably wouldn't even understand half of the jokes because they are related to headlines that we have all forgotten since then. It's almost as if every five minutes the world goes, "All right already, we've heard that one... tell us something NEW!"

As a youth speaker, these kinds of stories are the worst because they are so powerful but so short-lived. One November I was speaking at a high school in Oklahoma just a week or two after Halloween. Around the same time, a certain reality-television celebrity by the name of Kim Kardashian was in the news for getting married and divorced in a very short period of time.

So as an opener for my speech, I asked the crowd if they'd had a good Halloween, if any of them had dressed up as anything cool. Then I said, "I was going to be Kim Kardashian's marriage for Halloween, but I'm not short enough."

For whatever reason, they thought that was hilarious. The whole crowd completely lost it. It really got me off to a good start for the rest of the speech.

But afterwards, I realized I could never use that joke again. It was already about halfway through November, so pretty soon people would think it was weird if I started my speech with, "Did everybody have a good Halloween?" And by the time the NEXT Halloween rolled around, the Kim Kardashian joke would be so outdated that I would have to go back and explain it all over again, like I did here. It just wouldn't work.

It was a great joke, but I was only able to use it one time.

Not all stories are like that, though. Some stories are timeless. Some stories somehow manage to appeal to generation after generation after generation. We call these *the classics*. They're stories that have stood the test of time, stories that could be told in any era, to any group of people, and they would still be amazing.

I don't know about you, but I want the story of my life to be like that. I want it to be timeless. I want it to be told long after I'm gone.

See, anybody can get lucky by being in the right place at the right time. It doesn't take any skill to do that. There are certain people in life who are very successful (in terms of money and status) simply because they happened to be born in a certain time period, or to a certain family, or in a certain country. And it just so happened that being born in that time period, in that country, to that family, was a very fortunate occurrence.

Most reality television stars are like this (when I say "stars", I am using the term in the loosest possible sense). Most of these folks were simply lucky enough to live in an age where people can gain riches and fame by doing stupid things in front of a camera. And then they were lucky enough to have access to a camera.

At any other time in history, most reality television stars would have starved to death because they have absolutely no recognizable jobs skills of any kind. But in this brief window of ridiculousness, they are able to thrive.

Other people find success because their parents were rich, or they happened to buy the right lottery ticket or be the millionth customer or stumble across buried treasure. And don't get me wrong, I am happy for these people. If any of those things happened to me, I certainly wouldn't complain.

But I want my story to be more than that, too. I want to be able to say I didn't just *stumble* onto greatness. There are certain people out there who are able to find success no matter where they go, people who are able to make something out of nothing. I want to be one of those people.

I recently met a lady like this. In the past ten years she started a successful cookie company, left that to start a successful home construction business, then left that to start a successful nonprofit. In between all of those things she managed to find time to coordinate 13,000 volunteers for an episode of Extreme Home Makeover. And the reason I met her was because she wanted to meet to talk about a NEW project she's starting, helping young kids get an early start on living meaningful lives. It seems as though everything this lady touches turns out amazing.

I want to be like that. I want to be the kind of person who succeeds no matter where I am placed, what hardships I have, or what resources I am given. I want to be able to bring greatness to any situation I'm involved in. I want to bloom wherever I am planted.

But how do you do that? How do you actually become that kind of person?

I think it has a lot to do with what you surround yourself with, what you engage in and absorb. I think it has to do with the way you spend your time, the things you allow into your life.

You know that phrase, "You are what you eat"? It's kind of like that. You become like the things you consume.

If you constantly consume things that are short-lived and temporary, don't be surprised when nothing you do seems to last. If you are in the habit of always throwing out perfectly good stuff so that you can get the latest edition, don't be surprised when your own work is thrown out ten minutes after it's made.

On the other hand, if you consume timeless things, things that have survived for generations, that have stood for centuries, you will begin to absorb the qualities of those things, to soak in their permanence. And in the same way that eating real food dulls your taste for junk food, consuming timeless things will dull your taste for the temporary.

This includes things like reading classic literature, viewing ancient art and architecture, studying thinkers whose philosophies have lasted longer than the typical fifteen minutes.

As you consume these things, you'll find that the craziness of *More! More! More! Now! Now! Now!* doesn't appeal to you anymore. You'll find that you have better things to spend your time on, things that will actually matter ten years from now.

But that's not the only thing to consider. In addition to the whole temporary vs. permanent thing, there's the question of active and passive consumption.

Think about the things that influence you. Are they things you have to actively engage with, to wrestle with and question and push back against? Or are they best consumed passively, without question or interaction?

Most people practice passive forms of consumption. They watch a lot of television and listen to the radio and go to the movies. They listen to celebrity gossip and follow wherever culture leads them, never questioning or engaging in meaningful discussion about what influences them. They just sit back and absorb whatever comes their way. They are passive consumers.

Active consumption, on the other hand, involves things like reading, studying, learning and discussing. These are things that require you to engage your mind, to question and push back, to decide whether you will accept or reject an idea. They take effort and energy, and they can't be done in a glossy-eyed state, sprawled out across a couch somewhere with a bag of chips. Instead, they require focus, concentration, and energy. They require presence of mind and a willingness to engage.

They also require time, though. And that's the thing most people complain about.

Whenever I talk about this stuff, someone will inevitably say something like, "Reading?! Who has TIME for that?"

To which I respond "People who don't want to make minimum wage the rest of their lives! People who don't want to settle for whatever is handed to them! People who want to determine their own fate!"

But in reality, that answer is too long. The short answer is that we all have time for this stuff. How do I know? Because we have time for the things that matter to us. You might say, "My schedule is so full I couldn't fit anything else in if I wanted to!"

But it's not true. If I set a suitcase full of cash in front of you and said you could have it if you read a certain book, studied a certain subject, or learned a certain skill, you would magically find time in your schedule.

The irony is that if you did these things on your own, they would be worth far more over the course of your life than just one suitcase of cash. Far, far more.

If you truly don't have time though, there's an easy fix. It's as simple as swapping your passive forms of consumption for active ones.

In layman's terms? Turn off your electronics.

You might say, "There's nothing wrong with electronics, Kyle! Televisions and cell phones and computers aren't bad!" And you would be right. There's nothing intrinsically wrong with any of it. And there are certainly some redeeming qualities about all of these things. But the fact remains that they take up a lot of time. And most of the things we use electronics for don't make us any smarter.

You can argue with me all day and night, but I will always come back to this: the most amazing people I know, the ones with the best stories, are the ones who watch the least amounts of television, play the least amounts of video games, and spend the least amounts of time surfing the internet. It's not that they don't like these things, or that they don't understand the appeal of them. They simply have too many other things to do with their time. Better things. Things that will last.

When I was in high school, my youth pastor would say, "Show me your friends and I'll show you your future". His point was that if we surround ourselves with a certain type of people, it's almost inevitable that we will become that type of person. And he wasn't the only person who had this idea, either. In fact, there's a whole economic theory that says if you average the incomes of your five closest friends, the number you get will be pretty close to *your* income. It's scary, but it's generally pretty accurate.

The quickest way to get richer, then, is to hang out with richer people. Because as you do, you will begin to absorb their habits, their mindsets, their philosophies. And the flip side is true, too: The quickest way to get poorer is to hang out with poorer people.

The same thing is true of intellect. If you surround yourself with people who are smarter than you, you will become smarter by association. You will begin to pick up on the ideas and insights of your friends, begin to absorb their wisdom almost without trying. And if you surround yourself with people who are dumber than you, you will become dumber by default.

Not everyone has access to a squadron of brilliant thinkers, though. Not everyone can surround themselves with living, breathing geniuses around the clock. This is why we have books and blogs and interviews, things that put us in contact with the ideas and philosophies of great people, that allow us to rub up against their ways of thinking.

But these things only benefit us when we consume them actively, when we wrestle with them, question them, push back against them. They only work when we engage with them in meaningful ways.

They only work when we unplug our gadgets and get down to business.

# 12

## —— The Value of Stories ——

BUT WHY SHOULD WE DO ALL OF THIS? I mean, living better stories sounds fun, but is it really worth spending our lives on? Shouldn't we be more worried about doing things that will pay the bills and keep the lights on?

I suppose those are admirable goals. If for no other reason, it's difficult to read books in the dark, so paying your electrical bill is a good idea. And to do that, you need money.

But money is made when valuable things are created.

And stories *are* valuable things.

In fact, I think stories are one of the best investments you will ever make. Ever. In your entire life.

Think about it. Stories are the only thing with all of the following qualities:

1. *Good stories are free to make:* It doesn't cost any money to make a good story. It might cost money to do whatever you're doing in the story (going to

Disneyland or taking a challenging class or riding in a hot air balloon), but it might not (taking a walk through the woods, helping your son with his homework, learning a new language from a book at the library or watching the sunset with your wife). And even if it does, it doesn't cost money to keep the story forever. Can you imagine if you had to pay money every time you told your favorite story? I would be broke.

2. *Good stories are free to gather:* Not only is it free to keep your own stories, but it's free to gather other people's stories too. If I take something that someone else wrote and I publish it, I have to pay that person every time I sell a copy. But when I say "My friend told me this story, you've gotta hear it..." I don't have to pay them anything because stories are free to gather and share.

3. *Good stories don't wear out.* Like I said earlier, good stories are timeless. Most other investments wear out eventually. They rust or fall apart or burn down. Stories aren't like that, though. The best ones don't wear out at all. This is why we still tell stories about people who died decades or even centuries ago (Abraham Lincoln, George Washington, Socrates, Plato, Moses, Jesus, etc.). Their stories are still good.

4. *Good stories can't be stolen.* Yes, someone could "steal" your story and pretend it's their own. People who read this book could tell my story about prank-calling the President as if they were the ones who did it. But stories can't be stolen in the same way other things

116

are stolen. If I have five dollars and you steal it, I don't have it anymore. But if I have a story and you steal it, I still have it. I can still use it. And the story doesn't become less valuable by being stolen. It actually becomes *more* valuable to me because more people are hearing and sharing and spreading the story.

5. *Good stories don't take up space.* Every other investment takes up space. If you have a bunch of gold bars (If this is you, we should talk.), you have to get a giant safe or treasure chest. If you have tons of cash, you have to keep it in a bank somewhere. If you've got stocks and bonds, there are certificates and quarterly statements and other things you have to keep track of. But stories aren't like that. You can store them in books, I suppose, but you don't have to. They stay in your head, ready for use at a moment's notice.

Not only are all of these things true (and they are), but there's one more thing that *really* makes stories worthwhile.

6. *Good stories make everything they touch more valuable.*

What do I mean by this? Well, several things.

First of all, stories add social value. When you have a good story, you suddenly become more valuable to the people around you. If you have a *really* good story, people will actually stop what they are doing to hear you tell it. They will put down what they are working on, turn to you, and just listen.

That's body-language for, "What you are saying right now, the story you are telling, is more valuable to me than anything else I could be doing."

That might not seem like a big deal, but it is, because they are giving you their attention. And giving you their attention means giving you their time, which is the one resource they can never get more of.

This doesn't just work in small-scale social situations, either. It works with big crowds, too. Think about the last time you saw someone make a speech. If the speech was any good, it's probably because there were some stories in it. But here's the thing: most of the stories probably had nothing to do with the person giving the speech. Some of them were probably not even true, like parables or jokes or illustrations. But they made the speech better, more impacting, more resonant. They made the speech more powerful.

And because the speech was better, you valued the speaker more. You thought more of them because they gave a great speech.

You might think, "That's nice, but social value doesn't pay the bills." But you're wrong.

Did you know that most people don't get jobs by submitting résumés and job applications? It's true. Most people get jobs through their social connections, through knowing someone who knows someone who is looking to hire someone. These connections spring out of relationships, and relationships are built around shared stories.

Social value is also the reason why we go see movies with our favorite stars in them before we even know what the movie is about, why we buy books by our favorite authors without even reading the back cover. We place a higher social value on these people, which makes us more willing to spend money on the things they make, their movies and books and albums.

But stories can pay the bills in other ways, too. Stories themselves can add significant value to something simply by being associated with it.

A few years ago there was an experiment done to test this idea. A group of 100 creative writers got together and gathered 100 pieces of useless junk. These were items purchased from thrift stores and garage sales and secondhand shops, things that should have been thrown out but were instead donated.

None of the items cost more than $4, and most of the items cost right around $1.

Each writer was given one of the items. 100 writers, 100 items. Then each writer took his or her item and wrote a story about it.

That was the only instruction given: write a story about this item. It could be a funny story, a sad story, a happy story, a scary story, any story at all. It just had to be about the object they were given or involve it in some way.

Then they gathered all of the objects back together and put them on eBay.

Of course, the writers knew it is possible to add value to something by *lying*. For instance, you could find a weathered old baseball in the woods and say it belonged to Micky Mantle, or that Babe Ruth once licked it or something, and people might pay more money for it. But the writers didn't want to do that. They didn't want to be dishonest. So they put a disclaimer on each item saying that the story they were telling was not true, that it was made up to test whether or not a story will make something more valuable. They were very transparent with what they were trying to do.

They put the items on eBay with their stories attached, and they waited.

The initial value of those items, the cost to buy them all from the thrift stores and garage sales and secondhand shops, was $128.74.

The hypothesis was that tying stories to these items would increase their value. And it did. But by how much?

A little? More than a little?

Turns out, it was quite a bit.

When the dust settled and the last eBay auction ended, the grand total of the items sold was $3612.51.

Three thousand six hundred and twelve dollars! And fifty-one cents!

That means that each item became 28 times more valuable simply because a story was attached to it. A story that was admittedly not even true.

That's why I say stories are a great investment. If you put your money into a really aggressive mutual fund, you will be lucky to get a 10 or 15 per cent return on it. That means at the end of a year, your one dollar will be worth $1.10 or $1.15.

If you tie a story to that dollar, it becomes worth $28.00. Not too shabby.

You might think, "Okay, but that's one isolated example. I still don't buy the idea that stories add value to things."

Fair enough. But what about this: Have you ever heard of Oprah? Or Katie Couric? Or Matt Lauer? Or Diane

Sawyer? Or Anderson Cooper? Or Jon Stewart? Or Stephen Colbert? How about Conan O'Brien or Jay Leno or David Letterman?

These people are not famous for the things they have done. They haven't been elected president or climbed Mount Everest or survived a plane crash, haven't made a hit movie or recorded a number one song. But you know what they've done instead? They have found people who have done all of these things, and they have told their stories.

They've interviewed them, asked them questions, pulled out details and quotes, dug deeper to get more information. They are expert storytellers, professionals in the art of communicating other people's stories. And because they are good at it, we pay them millions and millions of dollars.

They all have different approaches, different ways they get it done. Some, like Oprah or Diane Sawyer, take a more serious approach. Others, like Conan O'Brien or Jon Stewart or Stephen Colbert, are a bit more lighthearted. But they are storytellers nonetheless.

If those examples don't convince you of the value of stories, consider this: this book, the one you are reading right now, is full of stories. Many of them are not even mine. They are stories I read about or heard from other people or saw in a movie. I got them for free, but people (like you, or whoever bought this book for you) pay to read them. And when I travel and speak to groups across the country, I get paid to tell those stories again and again.

I make my living telling stories. Every time I live another good one, it's like money in the bank for me because I know I will be able to tell it later onstage or in a book, to share and spread that story and get paid for it.

The same is true for you, regardless of your line of work. No matter what you do for a living, the things you experience, the places you go, the stories you live through... all of these things will make you more valuable because they'll give you the experience necessary to tackle whatever problems come your way.

Like I said before, money isn't everything. But if you are going to have to pay the bills anyway, you might as well have fun along the way, right? You might as well get paid for your stories.

# 13

## —— Tribute Band Groupies ——

NOT ALL STORIES ARE VALUABLE THOUGH. If you want to end up with valuable stories, you are going to have to have the kinds of experiences that will be worth something down the road.

A friend of mine recently took in some old video games to sell, games he hadn't played in years. He had one game in particular he thought would be worth some money because it had been very popular when it came out.

But when he showed it to the guy at the game store, the guy wouldn't even buy it. He pointed to a shelf behind him where he had about a hundred copies of the exact same game.

"I don't need this one, man. I need the ones nobody thought to buy when they were available."

I know it's ridiculous, but that struck me as pretty profound because I had been thinking about all of this story stuff around the same time.

It turns out experiences are the same way. If you've got

the same ones as everyone else, don't be surprised when nobody wants to hear your stories, when nobody thinks you have lived an interesting life. It's not that they don't like you, it's just that they can hear those stories anywhere.

If you want to have valuable experiences later, you need to be living the stories nobody else is living now, doing the things no one else is thinking to do yet, the things that will be valuable ten years down the road.

When you read stories of great people, people who have done amazing things and changed the world, you almost always find some degree of outsider status in the early parts of their lives, a sense that they didn't quite fit in with everyone else. And it's usually because they were interested in different things, things the other kids didn't fully understand or appreciate yet. It was only later in life, when the others were just getting started trying to do something worthwhile with their lives, that they began to appreciate the kids who had been doing these things all along.

I always thought it would be funny to get a bunch of people to camp out for a movie nobody cares about, one that will probably only be in theaters for a week or two, something with Nicolas Cage in it. We would do the whole deal, too: set up tents in a line, bring food and supplies, maybe even dress up as characters from the movie. I figure if nothing else it would probably get us on the local news or something.

Obviously the joke would be that there's no need to camp out. You could walk up and buy tickets at any point because there would be no real demand for them. We would be poking fun at the ridiculousness of getting so excited for something that will be so quickly forgotten.

When you are in junior high and high school, the world you are in seems so real, so complete and self-contained, as though the things that happen within the walls of your school and the bounds of your community are the only real things, the only things that matter. The outside world is recognized and even interacted with, but it's ultimately not that important in the day-to-day. The fact that there are large numbers of people outside your school who would love and accept you, who would be excited about the things you are doing and the dreams you are working to achieve, doesn't really make much of a difference if none of those people are in your life now.

But once you get out of that bubble, out into college and the real world, you find that the things that were important in high school and junior high are not important anymore. Athletic status and who-is-dating-who are not things people spend a lot of time thinking about when they are working on building a legacy. The he-said-she-said world of adolescent gossip is forgotten as quickly as the movies that aren't worth camping out for.

I live about an hour away from a town called Branson, Missouri. Branson calls itself the family-friendly Las Vegas, but it's really just a place where country musicians instinctively go to die, like an elephant graveyard. In the past few years though, other types of performers have started doing shows in Branson, too. There's a group of singing, dancing Irishmen (Not leprechauns though. I looked into it.), a group of Chinese acrobats, and even a place where people ride trick horses and an ostrich through an arena while you are eating dinner. I'm not kidding.

But the one category of shows that baffles me the most is that of the tribute band.

Tribute bands are groups that only exist to play another band's songs. They don't play anything original, anything they wrote themselves, anything they slaved over at three in the morning, scribbling lyrics on the back of an envelope in a hotel room somewhere as tears poured down their cheeks. Instead, they play songs another band wrote and performed and made popular, often years or even decades earlier.

There are several bands like this in Branson. There's a Beatles tribute band that has its own theater, and they play a whole show every night full of Beatles songs. They even wear the sort of outfits the Beatles used to wear and have wigs to make them look like the Beatles (or at least like people who are desperately trying to look like the Beatles).

But they're not the Beatles.

There's another theater where they have a whole group of musical impersonators, people who imitate Elvis or Buddy Holly. But the weird thing is, they also have impersonators of people who are still alive, people like Garth Brooks and Alan Jackson, guys who are still traveling and performing their own shows to stadiums full of fans.

That seems weird to me.

But to me, the thing that stands out most about tribute

bands and impersonators is this: they don't have groupies.

All the performers they imitate were immensely popular in their day, with crowds of raving fans who would follow them around the country and scream when they walked onstage. All of these groups had to have big entourages with security and personal bodyguards to keep fans at a distance.

But the impersonators don't need any of this. Nobody follows them around, no one gets excited when they see them in the mall, teenage girls do not throw themselves on the ground in a fit of excitement when they walk by. No one seems to care very much at all.

I know this because I once played a game of pickup basketball with an Alan Jackson impersonator at a local fitness center, and no one seemed to be very impressed when I told that story the next day.

These tribute bands and impersonators are living someone else's story. They are riding the coattails of someone else's success. And sometimes it works. Sometimes they do well. If nothing else, they have been able to make a living from it. But I can't imagine it would be very fulfilling. I can't imagine the applause would really mean that much, because the audience is not really applauding you. They're applauding the thought of someone else, the memory of someone who you sort of resemble when you wear that ridiculous wig, someone who they used to love but couldn't afford tickets to see.

You are simply playing a part for them, like an actor in a play.

When I travel to schools to give talks, I notice that a lot

of the students seem to be playing parts too, like there was a script that got sent around to all the schools and tryouts were held.

It's the same script for every school. There's the popular jock who is a big jerk to everyone, but nobody stands up to him. There's his girlfriend, who is usually the captain of the cheerleading squad or the leader of the social elite or something, who looks down her nose at people who dress or act or think differently, whose closest friends secretly hate her but desperately crave her approval. There's the sporty soccer chick who's too cool for a boyfriend, the nerdy fat kid with a heart of gold, the class clown who doesn't apply himself... the list goes on.

It's almost as if there is a grid made for these stereotypes, and everyone is assigned a spot on the grid, told to stay put and play their part.

But the truth is, people who fit into grids are replaceable. If you take any of those students and remove them from their position, either because they graduate or drop out or move to a different school, someone will inevitably come in and fill that slot. The system can't function without the key players, so it creates a sort of vacuum that sucks in the next viable candidate.

If you can fit into a grid or be defined by a stereotype, if your life closely resembles any of the characters on a teen television show or movie, then you are playing a role, a part that anyone could play. You are a member of a crappy tribute band, playing someone else's songs instead of stepping out with your own material.

And when you leave, someone else will fill your spot.

You deserve better than that. You should be living a life

that is irreplaceable, telling a story that can't fit on a grid or line up with a stereotype. When you leave, there should be a giant hole, miles outside of the grid, that no one but you can fill.

My friend was disappointed to find that his video game was worthless, a victim of its own popularity. But he should have known the most valuable things in life are the rare things, the hard-to-find things, the one-in-a-million things.

Don't be afraid to be one of those things. Don't be afraid to be unique, to be one-of-a-kind.

I am not saying you should be weird for the sake of weirdness, but I *am* saying you should not be afraid to be yourself. Develop your own interests, your own personality, your own identity, regardless of what other people are saying or doing or thinking. Define your life the way you want to define it. Tell the story you want to tell.

And if you're on the grid now, don't sweat. There's still time to escape. That's the thing about great stories: they change. They evolve. They develop.

If you don't like where you're at, change it. If you don't like the story you're telling, throw it away and start telling a better one.

The best thing you can do is to realize that the grid lines never existed anyway. They're imaginary.

Ignore the lines. You can go wherever you want.

# 14

## —— The Floor is Lava ——

ONE OF MY FAVORITE MOVIES OF ALL TIME IS a film called *The Brothers Bloom*. It's the story of two brothers who were gentlemen thieves. They traveled the world having all sorts of crazy adventures and living out these elaborate stories they'd made up.

In one scene one of the brothers is having a conversation with a girl named Penelope, and he finds out Penelope was trapped inside her house for 20 years.

What happened was this: when Penelope was young, she had an allergic reaction to something, but the doctors weren't sure what it was. So they did a test where they drew a grid on her back and then pricked her with needles full of diluted toxins, things that people can be allergic to. They told her to come back the next day, and if anything had swollen up they would know they had found the allergy.

When she came back though, her whole back was swollen, a disgusting mess of nasty red lumps.

The doctors informed her that she was allergic to just

about everything. They told her she should stay inside at all times or else risk having a deadly reaction if she came across any of these allergens in the outside world. Hearing this, her parents kept her inside and sealed off the house with plastic, installing a special air filtration system and everything.

Years went by, and one day the doctors came back. They told Penelope they had made a terrible mistake, that she was not allergic to any of the things they'd tested. Rather, she was allergic to the particular aluminum alloy the needles had been made of. She had spent all that time trapped in her house for nothing.

When Penelope is telling this story, the guy asks her how she handled it, how she kept from going crazy being trapped inside for all those years.

I'll never forget her answer. She said, "I decided this wasn't a story about a miserable girl trapped in a house.... This was a story about a girl who could find infinite beauty in anything."

Then she said, "I told myself that story until it became true."

So for all those years she was trapped in the house, she decided to learn anything she could.

She learned how to play the piano, how to play the guitar and the harp and the banjo and the violin.

She learned how to do gymnastics and ride a skateboard.

She learned how to do pinhole photography.

She learned how to juggle. She learned how to ride a unicycle.

She even learned how to juggle while riding a unicycle.

She learned all sorts of different stuff, probably more

than most people who *weren't* trapped in a house that whole time.

I always loved that story because it shows the power of a changed perspective.

Most people in that situation would have been given to despair over the boundaries in place, the four walls of the house that could not be escaped. Penelope, though, saw it differently.

Rather than thinking of all the things she could not get *out* of the house (namely herself), she thought of all the things that she could get *into* the house, things she could learn and do and master.

I wonder how our lives would be different if we thought of things the same way. Most of us won't be trapped in a house for twenty years, but we all have boundaries in our lives, things that prevent us from doing certain things or going certain places.

Some of these boundaries have to do with your bank account. If you are poor, you won't have the resources to go everywhere you want to go in the world. You will be limited to certain places until you are able to get some more money.

Other boundaries are related to status. If you are just an average Joe, the Secret Service is not going to appreciate you trying to get into the President's office for a friendly chat, even if you have some really good ideas. That's going to be outside of your boundaries. Or perhaps you are an American and you have always dreamed of hiking through the luscious hills of North Korea. Good luck with that.

Some boundaries are related to time. Even if you have all of the money and power in the world, you will never have enough time in your life to see everything there is to see on the earth. You will have tomiss out on certain places simply because there is not enough time to see them.

Whatever your boundaries are, you can whine about the fact that they exist, that you can't get outside of them, or you can spend your time bringing things in from the outside, filling your boundaries with beautiful, meaningful stories. Personally, I would rather do that.

Of course, all of this is assuming that your boundaries are even real. They may not be as real as you think.

When you were a kid, did you ever play that game where you pretended the floor was lava, that the walls were poisonous vines or made of fire? And you had to get from one place to another without touching any of it?

That was a fun game until someone else walked in, someone who wasn't playing the game and didn't like pretending, usually someone's older sister. She would walk into the middle of the room and you would scream, "Watch out, the floor is *lava!*"

Then she would look at you like you were an idiot and she would keep on walking.

As much as I hated those people for ruining the game, I think they had a pretty sound philosophy for how you should live your life: Look at the things people are spending their time and energy freaking out about, and ask, "Is this real? Is this worth the hysteria?"

Usually you'll find that it's not, that the floor is just a regular carpet and the walls are fine too.

There was an experiment done years ago where scientists placed some monkeys in a cage, and they placed some bananas near the top of the cage. Whenever the monkeys tried to climb up to get the bananas, the scientists would spray the monkeys with ice-cold water from a fire hose.

They didn't spray the climbing monkey though. They sprayed the ones who were chilling out in the bottom of the cage minding their own business.

Pretty soon the monkeys got tired of being sprayed, so whenever one of their fellow monkeys tried to climb up to get the bananas, the other monkeys would pull him back down and beat him up before he could get high enough to get them all soaked.

Then one at a time, the scientists started swapping out the old monkeys with new ones. And when the new monkeys tried to climb up to get the bananas, their fellow monkeys beat them up before they got high enough to get sprayed. They got the idea pretty quick.

Pretty soon all of the original monkeys, the ones who had been there for the actual spraying, had been swapped out for new monkeys. None of these monkeys had any idea why they couldn't climb up to the bananas because they hadn't seen the fire hose, hadn't been sprayed even once. But the behavior had been picked up, so they continued to beat each other up whenever one of them tried to get the bananas.

A lot of things in life are like this. At one time, there was a good reason for doing them, just like at one time the monkeys were smart to pull their friends back down (Perhaps the violent beatings were unnecessary, but hey... it's a monkey-beat-monkey world out there).

But now the danger is gone, the fire hose has been put away, and we are still holding on to the same behaviors.

At one time, even recently, the only way to be guaranteed a good job was to go to college. There were a few guys who found a way to make money without it, but by and large college was your ticket to success.

But now things are changing. Now there are lots of people who have college degrees and have killed thousands of trees sending out résumés but still haven't gotten a single job offer. These aren't delinquents, either. These are people who did well in college and did all of the things they were supposed to do.

And then on the flip side, you've got more and more people who are bypassing the college route altogether in favor of self-education or entrepreneurship or something else entirely.

I know a guy named Keegan who did this. Keegan is a very talented graphic designer. He started learning Photoshop and Illustrator and all of that when he was very young. By the time he was 16 he had landed a full-time job doing graphic design work (he was home schooled, so he made it work).

When Keegan finished high school, he started looking into college options. He wanted to study graphic design because that's what he loves. But he didn't end up going to college. You know why?

One day one of Keegan's friends, a guy who was taking graphic design classes in college, called Keegan. "You'll never believe this." he said. "Today our teacher was pulling up examples of great design work, and he was using things that you had created. He was pulling stuff from your website."

Keegan decided that if the college professors were taking cues from him, it didn't make sense for him to go to college.

So he didn't. He went and got a great job doing what he loves, and he is constantly teaching himself how to be better at it. And I think it's working out for him. He just got hired by Facebook.

Don't get me wrong: there's nothing wrong with going to college. But if you go thinking you will be guaranteed a job, or even a good education, you may be disappointed. The world is changing.

The truth is, many people are playing by rules that are outdated, rules that were created for a world that doesn't exist anymore. It's not their fault though. They're just playing by the rules they learned, playing within the boundaries they were taught to play within. It's just that those boundaries don't exist anymore. The rules have all changed.

And sometimes, the rules have been thrown out altogether.

Today there are high school students who are millionaires before they even graduate. There are middle-schoolers starting their own tech companies, hiring people their parents' age. There are even retirees reinventing themselves, starting fresh after decades in a different career.

The rules have completely changed. And if you aren't aware of this, you'll be pulled down by people who are still afraid of the ice-cold water from the fire hose.

But even if the rules are still in place, it's not so bad.

What's the worst thing that could happen to the monkeys? They get a little wet? They're *monkeys!* They live in a cage all day. It's not like they have anything better to do. Maybe the water will spice up an otherwise boring day. Or maybe it will wash away the nasty monkey smell.

For you and me, the consequences usually aren't so bad either, even when the rules prove to be true.

We spend so much time holding back, afraid to step out and try something new. But what are we afraid of? Oftentimes if we really think about it, the worst thing that could happen is someone could laugh at us, someone could reject our ideas or tell us we are stupid.

Is that really so bad? Are those people really so important to us, their opinions so valuable, that we would throw away our dreams and ambitions because of what they might think?

I don't think so.

I say it's better to risk it. If it turns out well, you'll be glad you stepped out of your comfort zone. And even if it doesn't, you'll pick yourself up, dust off, and try again.

You'll be just fine.

# 15

## — Choose Your Own Adventure —

SOMETIMES YOU'RE NOT THE ONLY ONE TRYING to tell a story about your life. Sometimes you will find that other people are telling stories about you too.

For as long as I can remember, people have had opinions about how my life was going to turn out. And for the most part, these opinions have fallen into two categories, two stories that I have heard people tell about me again and again.

The first one is, "You're going to be a millionaire someday, Kyle."

People said this from the time I was a kid because I was always scheming, always coming up with new business ideas, new ways to make money or raise funds for a project.

When I was in grade school, my younger brother and I started a business selling earthworms. We would pick up the worms in our yard after it rained, keep them in a giant pickle jar, and sell them to fishermen to use as bait.

Well, *in theory* we would sell them to fishermen. In reality, we never sold a single worm. Looking back, I think the fact that we lived on a dead end road that was an hour away from the nearest fishing spot may have hurt our business. We hadn't really thought through the challenges of our location.

The worms were doomed, too. Now that I think about it, I am pretty sure my parents still have a jar full of dead worms and dirt in their garage somewhere.

Oops.

Later, when I got to middle school, my best friend and I decided we were going to build a series of theme parks that would make us filthy rich. We would be so rich that we would each have houses in all fifty states, and in each state we would build our houses right next to each other with a secret tunnel connecting them so we could hang out all the time.

We drew up diagrams of all the rides, of the roller coasters and water slides and play areas for little kids who weren't tall enough for the cool stuff. We decided on the menus for the concession stands, picked out the souvenirs we would sell and figured out how much tickets would cost. Sometimes we would even draw plans for our houses with the secret tunnels connecting them.

But then we found out how much it costs to build a theme park. Let me tell you, it's not cheap. It was slightly more than we had anticipated, to say the least. We added it up, and even if we had combined our allowances, it would have taken us about a million years just to build the first ride. Our dream of owning and operating theme parks (and more importantly, our dream of being filthy rich and owning fifty sets of interconnected houses) was washed down the drain.

So far I was responsible for two failed businesses. This was not a good start.

I finally managed to make some money when I started designing tee shirts and selling them to friends in high school. The shirts were pretty ridiculous and said things like "Name-calling is for sissies" or "What's so safe about a safety pin?"

I would bring the shirts to school and sell them out of my locker or the trunk of my car or out of my backpack before class. But when the school administration found out about it, I got called down to the office for a friendly visit.

"You need to stop selling tee shirts at school." said the Vice-Principal.

"Why?" I asked. "Is there a rule against selling tee shirts at school? I didn't see one in the handbook."

"You can't be running a business on school property, Mr. Scheele," she told me.

"Oh." I said. This sounded like it was probably true.

So I asked the next logical question.

"Just out of curiosity, where *exactly* does school property end?"

From then on, all transactions were conducted on the street that ran next to the school. Once there was a break in traffic we would step into the street. I'd take the money, they'd take the shirt, and we would step back onto school property once the transaction was finished. It was a pretty great system.

This was only one of the ways I raised money in high school though. Once, I decided I needed a hundred bucks to buy a gorilla suit to wear to a football game. But "I want to buy a gorilla suit to wear to a football game" was too long, so I made a sign that said *"The Coolest Thing Ever"* and taped it to a coffee can.

I went around at lunch asking people, "Would you like to donate to the coolest thing ever?"

"What is it?" they would ask.

"It's the coolest thing ever." I would say.

I raised thirty-five bucks in twenty minutes before the principal made me stop.

Things like this were the reason that people said, "You're going to be a millionaire someday, Kyle."

But they weren't the only ones with predictions about my future. There was another thing that I heard a lot, too.

"Somebody is going to beat you up one day, kid."

People said this because I was always a little mouthy. If you haven't picked up on it already, I tend to enjoy the use of sarcasm from time to time. This used to get me into trouble with people who did not enjoy that kind of humor, particularly when it was aimed at them or referenced the physical attractiveness of their mother.

I was never trying to offend anyone (okay, I was *rarely* trying to offend anyone), but occasionally I would say the wrong thing to the wrong person and have to apologize. People assumed that one day I would go a little too far, that I would create the perfect storm of saying the wrong thing to the wrong person at the wrong time, and as a result I would end up getting my face smashed in.

For the record, it never happened. So far my face remains entirely un-smashed. I've never even been in a fight, actually. And I think I've learned to control the things I say now so that it will never happen. Hopefully.

It was interesting having these things said about me though because they were so vastly different. On one hand you had people predicting great success, and on the other hand, great failure (or at least great injury).

When I think about it, one group was focusing entirely on my strengths, like creativity and entrepreneurship, while the other focused on my weaknesses, like speaking before thinking or being rash.

These two groups were telling completely different stories about me and my life and how it would turn out. And it was up to me to decide which story I was going to listen to.

If I listened to the group who said I'd be a millionaire, it would give me more confidence, more boldness, a stronger belief in myself. I would be more willing to try new things and believe they would work out in the end because so many other people believed in me.

If I listened to the second group though, things would have turned out a lot differently. Instead of reaching out, I would have shut down, shut up, and lost my edge. I would have lived in fear of getting my face smashed in, and that fear would have choked out any boldness or ingenuity. It's hard to think of good ideas when you're constantly worried about someone beating you up.

In the end, I decided to ignore the naysayers and listen to the people who believed in me. I decided I would grow into my strengths and out of my weaknesses. Not only that, but I could probably turn the weakness into a strength anyways. In reality, the mouthiness I had was simply boldness that needed to be channeled into something more productive.

So far it's worked out. I'm not a millionaire yet, but I'm really not worried about it. That was never the goal. But knowing that other people think I could be a millionaire has given me the confidence to start a successful speaking business, design an iPhone app, and even write this book.

And as I mentioned, I have yet to have my face smashed in.

In your life, people will tell all kinds of stories about you too, about the kind of person you are and the kind of person you will be.

Some will say you're too much of a dreamer, that you should get your head out of the clouds. They'll say your ideas are unrealistic, that they'll never work in the real world.

And they may be right. Maybe some of your ideas are a little far-fetched. Maybe you do need to be more aware of reality. But listening to their advice probably isn't going to do that for you - It's just going to make you depressed. It's going to cause you to doubt yourself, to lose confidence in your ideas, and eventually it will cause you to give up altogether. Following their advice is not going to lead you to happiness or a better story.

On the other hand, you will have people telling you that you can do whatever you want, that the sky is the limit for you. They'll talk about the potential they see in you and say things like, "If I had *half* the creativity you have...."

The irony is that these people are the ones who are

actually wrong, at least from a technical standpoint. In reality you *can't* do everything you want because some of those things will violate the laws of physics — or the laws of your country. But that's not the point. The point is that by listening to these people you will be inspired to live a better story. You'll believe you can overcome the obstacles in front of you because of the special qualities that make you who you are.

For some of you, these stories won't be told by your peers, but by your parents and teachers. You may hear things like, "Your grandpa was a doctor, your father was a doctor, and if know what's good for you, you are going to be a doctor too." Or you may hear, "Son, I want you to have the sorts of opportunities I never had, so I'm sending you to law school. You're going to make something of yourself."

These are the hardest stories of all to shake because they have authority behind them. But you have to do it if you want a great story. If your parents want you to be a doctor or a lawyer but you have no interest in medicine or law, you are not going to be any good at what you do. You won't have the interest or the passion, which is what it really takes to be good at anything. At the very best you will be mediocre, and that doesn't do much for the family name.

These are tough conversations, but you have to be willing to have them. If you are going to live a truly great story, it has to be your own. You can't just read a script that someone else hands you.

When I was a kid, I used to read these books called *Choose Your Own Adventure!*

They were like regular books, except as you were reading there would be a page that said something like, "You come upon a dark and scary cave. To enter the cave, go to page 110. To turn and run, go to page 115."

Depending on which way you went, the story would turn out a different way. You might think there is a monster in the cave, but actually there's a chest of gold coins. Or you might think it is safer to turn and run, but when you turn to page 115 you find that you tripped and fell on a rattlesnake and died.

I loved these stories, but I didn't like the uncertainty of not knowing if I had chosen the right option. So I cheated. I wanted to make the story turn out the best way possible, so I would turn to both pages and read both sets of options. And once I saw how things would turn out, I would pick the one I liked better.

You should cheat too. When people tell stories about you, when they make predictions about how your life is going to turn out, flip ahead a few pages. Imagine how your life will change if you listen to their predictions, how it will affect your attitude and your outlook. If you like the change, go with that story. If you don't, ignore it.

It's a pretty simple way of living your life, but it works. And if you are smart about it, it just might keep you from falling on a rattlesnake and dying in the woods.

# 16

## —— Urban Legends ——

SINCE OTHER PEOPLE ARE GOING TO TELL untrue stories about you, it's only fair that you should be able to tell a few untrue stories about yourself every now and then. It's too much fun not to.

For instance, I once convinced my friend Jessica, whom I had known for years, that I was color blind. We were working together at a summer camp and had just taken our campers to a horseback riding session for the afternoon. I was telling her about the time I got kicked in the head by a horse when I was little (which is actually true), and after showing her the scar I said "The doctors think that's probably when I became color blind."

I wish I could say I just made it up on the spot, but I didn't. It had all started several months earlier when a friend of mine told me *he* was color blind, and I didn't know whether or not to believe him. How do you even prove something like that? So I figured I would see how hard it was to convince someone that *I* was colorblind, and perhaps that would help me decide whether my friend was lying or not (It turns out he was telling the truth. Sorry for doubting you, Kory).

"I didn't know you were color blind!" Jessica said, looking surprised.

"Yeah. I thought you knew?" I said.

"Is it all colors or just some?" she asked.

"All of them, I think." I said. "All I know is that I can't tell the difference between color photos and black and white ones. They all look the same to me."

"That's so crazy, Kyle! I can't believe I've known you for this long and you never mentioned this." she said.

"Well, I've been like this as long as I can remember, so it's not really weird for me. I guess I just never really think about it." I said.

"I guess that makes sense." she said.

I wanted to see how long I could keep this going, but I knew it would take a team effort to keep her fooled. As soon as we got back with the rest of the counselors, I pulled one of them aside and quickly whispered "If Jessica asks, I'm color blind. I'll explain later."

The girl just rolled her eyes and laughed, but she agreed to go along with it. I quickly spread the word to all of the staff, and everyone agreed to help.

For the next three days, Jessica kept asking me, "What color is this?" and I would say "I don't know... grey?" and she'd shake her head as if to say *Poor, poor Kyle... He can't even see colors.*

"What about this?" she'd ask.

"Umm... kind of a darker grey than the other one?" I'd say.

But on the third morning, I slipped up. I had not slept well the night before, and I hadn't had time to get coffee yet, so I was not exactly alert or even entirely conscious. As the entire camp lined up for our morning flag ceremony, Jessica leaned over and whispered, "Hey Kyle, what color is my shirt?"

Forgetting all about the elaborate web of lies I had so carefully spun, I gave her a weird look and said, "Red, why?"

I was about halfway through the word "why" when I realized what I had done.

I tried to recover. "Red, why.......why, it's a MIRACLE!" I shouted, opening my eyes wide as if I had just won the lottery.

But Jessica didn't buy it. She turned and stomped off into the dining hall and subsequently avoided me until I apologized.

Like I said though, I wasn't alone in this. I had help. I had to, or else it wouldn't have worked. By myself, it would have been impossible to keep the ruse going, but with a group of co-conspirators, anything is possible.

The fact is, the more people that believe something, the less other people will question whether or not it's true. *Surely this many people couldn't be wrong*, they think.

It's almost like an ideological form of peer pressure.

Peer pressure is a concept that gets tossed around a lot, usually in relation to drugs and alcohol and that sort of thing. And it certainly shows up there, so you should be aware of it. But those are the obvious instances of peer pressure, and they are avoided easily enough. It's the subtle ones you have to be careful about.

The subtler forms of peer pressure come when you hear something so many times that you automatically assume it is true, when so many people believe something that you absorb their belief subconsciously.

It's sort of like an urban legend. Urban legends are stories that aren't true, but enough people believe they are, and as a result they spread like wildfire. These stories pop up in our culture all the time, so much so that someone put together an enormous online catalog of them at snopes.com so you can see whether a particular story is true or not.

Snopes is great for stories about zombie hitchhikers and people getting stabbed with needles in movie theaters, but it isn't much use when it comes to the sorts of urban legends that pop up in our own personal stories, often in the form of "friendly advice".

My friend Jared deals with this on a daily basis. Jared is a bodybuilder and powerlifter. The dude is legit, too. At a recent competition, he squatted 850 lbs. That's not a typo. *Eight hundred and fifty pounds.* He also deadlifted 700 lbs and bench pressed 525 lbs. The man is a machine.

He is also one of the smartest guys I know when it comes to fitness. He has thoroughly studied everything he can about diet and exercise, about micro-nutrient balances and load progression and minor muscle group targeting and all of that. A couple of years ago I worked out with Jared for a few weeks and he had me lifting more weight than I had ever been able to lift before, simply because he showed me what I was doing wrong and put me on a smarter training schedule.

Jared has been studying the human body for as long

as I've known him, which is over ten years. Even when we were in high school, he was always reading books and magazines about lifting and bodybuilding. He knew what he wanted to do and he worked hard to learn everything he could about it.

But you know what still happens every time Jared goes into the gym? People give him workout advice. And it's always the same garbage, tips based on the urban legends of weightlifting, things that get passed around every gym in the world by guys who don't have any idea what they are talking about.

*You should do more reps, but use less weight.*

*You should do more weight, but fewer reps.*

*You should breathe more.*

*You shouldn't breathe so much.*

*You're gonna hurt yourself, man.*

And you know who's giving him this advice? Really fat guys and really skinny guys, guys who can't lift half as much as him, who haven't worked half as hard or for half as long, but who want to tell him what he should and shouldn't do because they once read an issue of *Men's Health* at the dentist's office.

Like I said, Jared's been doing this for over a decade. He's competed in events that you have to be *asked* to compete in. He's worked with some of the top guys in his field. He's a sponsored athlete who gets all of his supplements paid for.

The guy has clearly-defined abs at 250 lbs of body weight. He knows what he's doing.

But that doesn't stop the unsolicited advice from the

amateur squad. It doesn't stop the endless barrage of tips from guys who have no idea what they're talking about.

Luckily, Jared isn't dumb enough to listen to these guys. He knows what he's doing and he isn't deterred by people who don't. Jared can look at these guys and easily see (just based on their bodies vs. his) that they have no business giving him advice. Then he can get right back to the work he was doing, probably bench pressing a Volvo or something.

Jared isn't the only one who has to deal with this, though. Anytime a person tries to start living a better story, people come out of the woodwork with all sorts of advice.

*You're working too hard.*

*You're setting unrealistic expectations.*

*You need to slow down and enjoy life!*

*You've got too much stuff going on, man.*

And unlike Jared, who can simply look at the guy and determine whether or not his advice is any good, you and I can have a harder time discerning the good stuff.

I get this kind of advice quite a bit because I'm a very busy guy. I'm constantly coming up with new ideas, so I usually have several side projects going on. I'm up by 5 or 6 every morning and I often stay up late working into the night. So when I first started hearing these things, I thought, "Maybe they're right. Maybe I *should* slow down."

But I quickly became restless. I got bored, and I thought, "What do these people do with their free time?" So I asked them, and I found out they mostly watch TV and play video games. These are guys in their 20's and 30's, too.

As I dug deeper, I found out that was pretty much the extent of their non-work activities. They don't read, they aren't actively trying to learn any new skills, and they don't really have any long-term goals they're working toward.

As soon as I realized this, I got right back to work. I didn't (and don't) have any interest in that sort of lifestyle, so I shouldn't be taking advice from the sorts of people who are living it.

Since then, I've made a point to hang around people who are actively trying to make a dent in the universe, people with lofty goals and aspirations. And you know what I've found? None of them have told me to slow down. If anything, they've challenged me to reach for more.

As you step out and try to live a better story, people will give you advice, too. Some of it will be good advice that will save you time and money and heartache. But some of it will be junk, and it will do nothing but sidetrack you from the life you're trying to live.

Don't shut *everyone* out or you will be guaranteed to fail. But don't just take every bit of advice that comes your way, either. Consider the source. Ask yourself if you have any interest in living the kind of life this person lives. If not, don't waste your time following their advice. It won't get you where you want to go.

# 17

## —— Picking Fights ——

WHEN YOU BEGIN TO EXAMINE THE LIVES OF people who are giving you advice, it will depress you. You will start to see how many people are settling for a life that is *far* less than what it could be.

Henry David Thoreau said, "the mass of men lead lives of quiet desperation." And it's true. The vast majority of people sleep til the last possible second, rush to a job they hate, get stuck in traffic on the way home, sedate themselves with television, then go to bed so they can wake up the next day and do it all over again. They do this a few thousand times, then they die.

What a life, huh?

I used to be baffled by this. I couldn't understand why people would settle for this kind of existence. But now I know why: because living a better story is hard.

Living a better story involves struggle, conflict, a battle of some kind. In the movies it's always something obvious like a dragon or a killer alien army, or at least a really good football team. But for us the enemy isn't always so clearly defined. For us the enemy is usually a mindset, a habit, a persistent lethargy. And because of this, many people sit around waiting for a battle to fight, never realizing that the first enemy they have to overcome is their own laziness.

The hard truth is this: if you don't get in the habit of winning small battles, you will never be ready when the big ones come. This is why guys will talk all day long about what they would do if they witnessed a bank robbery, how they would tackle the robber and save the day. But how many times does this actually happen? Hardly ever. You know why? Because when people witness an actual bank robbery, they see a gun and think, "Maybe I'd better sit this one out..."

And because they aren't in the habit of overcoming fear and doing what needs to be done, they lay low and wait for the situation to resolve itself.

I'm not saying you should tackle guys with guns. In that situation, you're definitely better off just letting the guy take the money. But the analogy holds up for so many other situations.

You tell yourself you'll be the hero in a bank robbery because you know the odds of that scenario ever happening are incredibly slim. And by playing out the hero fantasy in your mind, you let yourself off the hook when it comes to actually doing the small, everyday things.

I don't play a lot of video games, but I've played enough to notice a pattern: You always start out having to beat a bunch of little bad guys, easy ones that die with just a single punch or kick or laser beam to the face. Then once you beat a bunch of those, you get to the level boss, who is a bit harder to kill. And once you beat enough of the level bosses, you get to the BIG BOSS at the end of the game.

If you take someone who has never played the game before and start them on the BIG BOSS level, they will inevitably lose. Over and over and over again. And then they'll give up and say it can't be done, that it's not possible.

But if you start them from the beginning and allow them to get some small victories, they'll gain confidence and experience. They will start to figure out what the buttons do and how to perform bonus ultra combo power-up moves for extra points. They'll start getting the hang of it, leaving a path of devastated bad guys lying in ruin behind them. And when they finally get to the big boss, they will beat him. Maybe not on the first try, maybe not on the second, but soon enough.

Life is the same way. If you don't take time to kill the little bad guys and end-of-level bosses, you will get in the habit of not fighting for the things you want. Then when the big boss comes along, you will be completely unprepared. The fight will be over before it even begins, and it won't end in your favor.

Depending on your outlook, this can either be good news or bad news. In reality, it's probably a little bit of both.

It's bad news because it means that you have more than one battle to fight. A lot more, actually. You may think you're fighting for the girl's heart, but in reality you've got to start by fighting to lose weight and get a job, and before you can do that you've got to fight to get up early and stop eating bags of corn chips all day.

But it's also good news because it means that the starting point is easier. You don't have to go out and win the girl's heart today. You aren't ready for that. All you have to do right now is get up and do a few push-ups. Go throw away all your junk food. Start there.

If your dream is worth anything, it is going to take a lot of steps to get there. There will be a lot of little battles along the way, a string of smaller wins and losses. But all you have to do right now is go fight the first one.

Maybe for you it's turning off your computer and reading a book. Or turning on your computer and looking online for someone to teach you Spanish. Or going to the library and checking out a book about how to draw unicorns. Or reaching out to someone you admire and inviting them to coffee.

This is the way that dreams are built: one small victory at a time.

If you need to lose 100 lbs, the worst thing you can do is say, "I'm going to lose 100 lbs!" because that number is so overwhelming that you'll give up as soon as you hit the first roadblock. Instead you should say, "All I've got to do is get up early tomorrow morning and take a walk. Not a run, not a jog, but a walk. That's all I'm committing to." Once you do that, you'll find it wasn't so bad. And the next day you'll do it again. The day after that you might actually eat some celery or something. And pretty soon you will realize you've lost ten pounds. Little by little you will build up bigger and better victories until you are running marathons and buying all new clothes. But it won't happen all at once. People who lose 100 lbs at once usually die.

When I decided to write this book, I took this idea into account. I knew if I just started writing I would be really motivated for the first couple chapters, and then I'd hit a rough patch and not know what to say next. Then I would probably give up. I knew this because it had happened before, and I still have the half-written books to prove it.

So instead of just saying, "I'm gonna write a book!" I brainstormed some topics. I went through several ideas, and I ended up narrowing it down to two. Then I started outlining. I got through several pages of one outline before I realized the idea wouldn't work. Perhaps it will make a good book in the future, but it isn't ready yet. So I put it aside and started outlining the second idea, this crazy thing about viewing your life as a story. And that idea seemed to come together, so I finished the entire outline from start to finish.

Then I expanded it, added more details and stories, took out parts I didn't like, made the whole thing stronger and more compelling. And when I was done with that, I showed it to some people I admire, people whose feedback would be valuable. I had them mark it up and question it and pick it apart. I had them give their unvarnished, completely honest opinions of it. Then I took their thoughts and went back to the outline, making changes where necessary.

And when all of that was done, I started writing. But even then, I didn't say, "Here I go! I'm going to write a book!" Instead, I woke up each day and said, "I'm going to write for an hour or two. If I get ten words or ten thousand, it doesn't matter. I'm just going to sit here and write until the time is up."

And so I did. And slowly, the book came together. And when I finished a draft, I sent it out to friends and family and even a few people who were almost complete strangers.

I asked for their feedback and they gave it to me. And based on that, I made changes. I added two chapters and removed two more. I took out stories that didn't fit and put others in their place. I took out several typos and probably put in a few by accident.

Then I started working on a cover design and a layout, started writing the introduction and the preface and all of the author's notes. I started thinking about acknowledgements and the back cover summary and author bio and all of that. Then one by one, I had small victories over each of these things.

And finally, I had a book. It took months of hard work, of small victories in battles against the alarm clock and the to-do list and a myriad of lesser priorities. It took longer than I thought and was harder than I had anticipated. But after winning a thousand tiny victories, I found that the great big final boss had already been killed.

I'd written a book. The same book you're holding right now, actually. Unless you are reading this in the bathtub, in which case you probably have it on one of those special stands so it won't get wet.

I've always wanted one of those.

# 18

## — Trust the Process —

IN THE END, THE BEST ADVICE I CAN GIVE YOU is this: trust the process.

The formula for living a great story is pretty simple: just keep doing the difficult things that are in front of you.

That's it. Do whatever difficult thing is in front of you, and when you've done that, do the next one.

When you fail, get up and try again. Dust yourself off, bandage your wounds, then get back to work.

Develop a habit of fighting for the things you want. Not just money and possessions, but time, relationships, freedom and legacy. Fight for these things until you get them, then fight even harder to keep them.

Inevitably, you will lose some of these battles. More than likely, you'll lose a lot of them. There will be times when it seems like you have lost a hundred in a row, when people around you will point and laugh and jeer. *Look at that fool. That's what happens when you try to do something big,* they'll say from the comfort of their recliners.

Don't listen to them. You are right where you're supposed to be.

The only way to guarantee failure is to quit. The only way to lose is to give up. But if you keep trying long enough and keep learning from your mistakes, you will win. I promise.

This is how the world works. It's how everyone you admire got to where they are.

If you dig into the history of your heroes you will find failure after failure after failure, interspersed periodically with a few minor successes. Then finally, after lots of ups and downs (during which it always feels like there are more downs than ups), people find a certain level of success. They catch their stride.

But people forget about these things. They forget about the embarrassments and the failures and the staggering losses.

People praised Steve Jobs for the iPhone and the iPad and for saving Apple from the brink of failure, but they often forget that he had a string of his own failures first, that he was laughed at and ridiculed and made fun of. If he had given up then, he would be nothing more than an obscure footnote in the historical record, just another person who failed to change the world. But he pressed on.

People praise their favorite actors and musicians, not knowing about the coffee shop concerts and community theater plays where they were terrible, where nobody came to see them and those that did left early.

We could go on and on down the list, but the formula holds up. Nobody who has a great story came by it easily. No one who has an amazing, adventurous life had it handed to them.

The same will be true for you. If you work as hard as you can for as long as you can, you will wind up with a good story. It will be extraordinarily tough, and you will be tempted to give up again and again and again. Many of the people who start out alongside you will give up along the way. They will buy comfortable chairs and put them in front of giant television sets and fall asleep watching other people's stories.

But not you. You'll keep going.

And after you have accumulated enough failures and rough drafts and rejection slips to build a mountain out of, you will find victory. You will catch your stride, and suddenly things will be easier.

People will forget about your failures, will write them off as though they never happened. They'll call you an overnight success because they weren't there to see the years of hard work that made it all possible.

And in that moment, you'll look back on it all and be glad that you did it. You will be glad you took that first step all those years ago, that you stepped out and gained a small victory. You will be glad you kept at it when others gave up. You will be glad you gave up your nights and your mornings and at times even your sanity, that you pushed through difficulty after difficulty until you rose above the clouds.

And then, once you've enjoyed your moment in the sun, you will quietly lower your head and get back to work because your story isn't finished.

Like I said, the best advice I can give you is this: trust the process.

You'll be glad you did.

# 19

## Conclusion

IN MANY WAYS, LIVING A BETTER STORY IS LIKE driving a new car: All of a sudden you begin to notice all of the other people that are driving the same kind of car. It's not that everyone bought one the same day you did, it's just that you never noticed until you had one of your own.

Personally, I am forever indebted to Donald Miller for introducing me to the concept of living better stories with his book *A Million Miles in a Thousand Years.* If you haven't read it, go buy it now. It is an incredible introduction to the idea of life as story, and it's written by an unbelievably gifted writer. You will be better for reading it.

Once I read that book, I began to see this concept everywhere. I began to run across it in books and magazines, in movies and real life. I began to see it in the lives of people I admired, people whose lives I wanted to emulate.

I even saw it in my own life, in the times where I had really lived, in the stories I found myself telling again and again. As I looked back on these times, I realized I had unknowingly drawn on the power of story myself.

I no longer do this by accident though. Now I go out of my way to seek out good stories because I want to live this out in every part of my life.

And because I want others to have good stories, I wrote this book.

None of this is groundbreaking or new. In fact, it's timeless. It's the only thing that works. I didn't discover it or improve on it. I simply observed it, commented on it, and added my own stories to the telling.

And now that you know it, you'll start seeing this play out in a million ways all around you too.

You will see many people settling for safety, for boring stories and a comfortable spot in front of the television.

You will see others start out trying for greatness, only to experience failure and give up.

And if you look hard enough, you will see people who fall down and get back up again. And again. And again and again and again. And eventually, you will see it all come together as their stories unfold into something they never would've imagined.

And then you'll go write a story of your own.

# SECTION 3

## Odds & Ends

# —— Would You Do Me a Favor? ——

People think you write books to make money, but that's a myth. The truth is, you write a book to get your message out to the world.

If you enjoyed this book, it would mean a lot if you would help me continue to get that message out. Here are three ways that would really help:

1. *Leave a review.*

Go to Amazon.com, search for "We Put a Man on the Moon", and leave a review. Say what you liked, say what you didn't. The more reviews a book has, the more people will check it out.

2. *Tell your friends.*

Instead of using your social media accounts to post pictures of sandwiches, why not post something useful, like, say, a quote from the book or a link to the Amazon page? Either one would be greatly appreciated.

3. *Email me.*

I'd *love* to hear your feedback. What did you love/hate? What made you want to take action? My email address is kyle@kylescheele.com. I read every email I get.

Of course, if you REALLY liked the book, you could always hire me to come give a speech to your school or organization. For more information on that, just turn the page.

# About the Author

Kyle Scheele is an award-winning author and speaker, although none of his awards have had anything to do with writing or speaking. In his life he has been awarded Employee of the Month, Camper of the Day, and has on many occasions been notified that he has won a prize for being the millionth visitor to a website, although he has had some difficulty in actually obtaining these prizes.

Kyle lives in Missouri with his beautiful wife Lindsay, their rambunctious son Wesley, and their adorable daughter Lucy.

Kyle speaks frequently on the topic of living better stories. He has given keynotes and workshops on this subject to thousands of teenagers across the United States at events ranging from school assemblies to student leadership conferences and everything in between. If you are interested in having Kyle come speak to your group, please contact:

*booking@kylescheele.com*

If you'd like to connect with Kyle, you can do so here:

*www.kylescheele.com*
*www.facebook.com/kylescheele*
*www.twitter.com/kylescheele*

# Acknowledgments

At the beginning of Chapter 1 I said, "Starting a book is hard." And that's true. But finishing one is even harder. And while it was my fingers that did the typing, this book was truly a group effort from start to finish. As such, I have a few people to thank.

First, my beautiful wife Lindsay. You believed in me when I'd never had a single speaking engagement. Thanks for letting me pursue this crazy dream, for encouraging me along the way, and for being the best wife and mother the world has ever known. I love you more and more each day.

Next, to Grant Baldwin. For helping me get my start in this business, for showing me the ropes, and for pushing me to do more than I thought possible - thank you. Writing this book was your idea, and I am forever grateful for your help along the way.

To Lisa Klug, who takes care of all of the planning details I would never even think about. You're the reason I am not lost somewhere in the middle of Philadelphia right now. Thanks for being awesome at what you do.

To my parents, who put up with my shenanigans through the years, kept me (mostly) out of trouble, and instilled in me the belief that anything is possible. I love you both more than you know.

To my brothers, Travis and Matt, whom I have fought both for and against more times than I care to count. You guys have both turned out to be pretty incredible guys, and I'm proud to say we're family.

To Mike Hall, Laymon Hicks, Jeff Yalden, Michael Cuestas, Josh Sundquist, Ryan Porter and all the other amazing speakers who have given me advice, listened to my crazy ideas, and encouraged me to keep this thing going. Your help means so much to me. This industry is truly like a family.

To my wonderful godmother Judy, who proofread the early drafts of this book and offered the hard feedback I needed to hear. Thanks for the tough love. This book is 100 times better because of you, and has about 100 fewer commas.

To Mr. Kinslow, who gave me a chance to make all my speaking mistakes early on, and who put up with more than he should have had to. Sorry for hiding in that coffin.

To John Lindell, Scotty Gibbons and Matt Blankenship, who believed I would turn out okay despite a preponderance of evidence to the contrary.

To Chris Lewis, who gave me my first real job despite the fact that I was extraordinarily underqualified, and who showed grace beyond measure when things didn't turn out the way we'd both hoped.

To Chris Mostyn, who did an excellent job on the cover art for this book and who has provided many hours of great conversation about art and life.

To the clients who hire me and the students I get to speak to. You are the reason I do what I do. Thanks for the kind words, the emails and facebook posts and tweets, and the laughter at appropriate times during the speech. You guys are awesome.

Last but not least, to my Kickstarter backers, who believed in this book when it was just a text file on a computer. Thanks for helping make this thing a reality, and for blowing my expectations out of the water. Your incredible support was more than I ever could have dreamed of.

As promised, the names of my Kickstarter backers are as follows (from first pledge to last): Laymon Hicks, David Messner, Tom Gebbie, Brandon Brandypants Cook, Ellie Schmelly Schmidly, William Newton, The Westhoff Family, Brooks Lockwood, Rod & Kim Whitlock, Elizabeth Alphonse, Dustin Ray, Ariahna Knight, Aunty Jenn, Brandon, Tyler, Lauren, Logan & Gabriel Johnson, Ian & Rachel VanHover, Ben Bennitt, Joe Keil, Luke & Amanda Cornwell, Brenton & Shelby Miles, Chuck Greenaway, Scott & Rose Schmidly, Erin Barcus, Petunia Petalpockets and her associate Huckleberry "Jazz Hands" Hufflebrow, Hans & Michelle Huo, Jonathan Roberts, Julie Higgins, Mitchell Dong, Nathan & Laura Mallonee, Gabrielle Guerra, Scott Wiskus, Brian & Angela Moody, Mason Jones, Jake Kohlmeyer, Griffin, Bethany, & Alby McGrath, Jeryd Lassley, Mikaela Minner, Jennifer Botts, Lisa Klug, Adam & Olivia Devizia, Tracy Whitcomb, John-Erik Moseler, Darian & Kristie Amsler, Captain Marshall & Donna Sherman, Susan & Victor Vergeer, Jason Vanderlaan, Caitlin & John Acker, Roy "The Easel Empire" Blumenthal, Richard Westerman, Holly Burtrum, Alex Bonnett, Dannah Nayblat, Danny Hoyt,

Ben Arment, Käte Lorimer, Allee Mixon, Jason & Aurelia Stratton, Jamie Bell, Hector Realubit & Jason Cox, Mike & Lynn Scheele, Sir Sean Luxton, Jim & Pam Blose, Dean Ferguson, Zach Metcalf, Lorena M., Danny Pettry II, Ron & Lisa Kohlman, Michael & Renae Cuestas, Anna N. Ureta, Vishwas Madhuvarshi, Josh Lorimer, Dave & Lisa Porch, Charlotte Jones, David Durham, The Mikel Howard, Gabriel Sebastian Jönsson, Dorothy P., Laura Vanessa Brown, Los Fentons, The Reverend & Mrs. Goeden, Heidi Suzanne Graves, Randy & Gina Smith, Phil & Susie Klapp, Drew Oglesby, Judy Johnson, Michael Gerber, Jennifer Piatchek Keith, Dugan & Ashley C., Joe M. & Jess S., D. Gilson, Kyle Kujala-Korpela, Matt Scheele, David & Becky Lindell, Mohammed M., Ricky Lorimer & Jaclyn Foehring Lorimer, Brandon Graves, Christopher James Howlett, Lorenzo Orselli, Myles Rhea Jefferson, Stephen & Katie Coppenwad, Mark & Julie Engelhardt, Margaret M. St. John, David & Tiffany Cumming, Stephen & Stephanie Maddox, Lauren Hiser, Cody & Erin Danastasio, Marloes Busscher, Lewis Goddard, Joe Chin, Max Cheng, Jim & Paula Kirk, Paul Clothier, & Zack Danger Green.

46557896R00098

Made in the USA
Charleston, SC
16 September 2015